About this Document

This report was developed by the Big Data Senior Steering Group (SSG). The Big Data SSG reports to the Subcommittee on Networking and Information Technology Research and Development (NITRD). The report is published by the Executive Office of the President, National Science and Technology Council.

About the Subcommittee on Networking and Information Technology Research and Development

The Subcommittee on Networking and Information Technology Research and Development is a body under the Committee on Technology (CoT) of the National Science and Technology Council (NSTC). The NITRD Subcommittee coordinates multiagency research and development programs to help assure continued U.S. leadership in networking and information technology, satisfy the needs of the Federal Government for advanced networking and information technology, and accelerate development and deployment of advanced networking and information technology. It also implements relevant provisions of the High-Performance Computing Act of 1991 (P.L. 102-194), as amended by the Next Generation Internet Research Act of 1998 (P. L. 105-305), and the America Creating Opportunities to Meaningfully Promote Excellence in Technology, Education and Science (COMPETES) Act of 2007 (P.L. 110-69). For more information, see www.nitrd.gov.

About the NITRD Big Data Senior Steering Group

The Big Data SSG was formed in 2011 to identify current Big Data research and development activities across the Federal Government, offer opportunities for coordination, and identify what the goal of a national initiative in this area would look like. Subsequently, in March 2012, The White House Big Data R&D Initiative was launched and the Big Data SSG continues to facilitate and further the goals of the Initiative.

Acknowledgments

This document was developed through the contributions of the NITRD Big Data SSG members and staff. A special thanks and appreciation to the core team of editors, writers, and reviewers: Lida Beninson (NSF), Quincy Brown (NSF), Elizabeth Burrows (NSF), Dana Hunter (NSF), Craig Jolley (USAID), Meredith Lee (DHS), Nishal Mohan (NSF), Chloe Poston (NSF), Renata Rawlings-Goss (NSF), Carly Robinson (DOE Science), Alejandro Suarez (NSF), Martin Wiener (NSF), and Fen Zhao (NSF).

Copyright Information

This is a work of the U.S. Government and is in the public domain. It may be freely distributed, copied, and translated; acknowledgment of publication by the National Coordination Office for Networking and Information Technology Research and Development (NITRD/NCO) is appreciated. Any translation should include a disclaimer that the accuracy of the translation is the responsibility of the translator and not the NITRD/NCO. It is requested that a copy of any translation be sent to the NITRD/NCO.

Subcommittee

on

Networking and Information Technology Research and Development

James Kurose, Co-Chair, NSF
Keith Marzullo, Co-Chair, NCO

NITRD Member Agencies

Department of Commerce
National Institute of Standards and Technology (NIST)
National Oceanic and Atmospheric Administration (NOAA)

Department of Defense
Defense Advanced Research Projects Agency (DARPA)
National Security Agency (NSA)
Office of the Secretary of Defense (OSD)
Service Research Organizations (Air Force, Army, Navy)

Department of Energy
National Nuclear Security Administration (NNSA)
Office of Electricity Delivery and Energy Reliability (OE)
Office of Science (SC)

Department of Health and Human Services
Agency for Healthcare Research and Quality (AHRQ)
National Institutes of Health (NIH)
Office of the National Coordinator for Health Information Technology (ONC)

Independent Agencies
Department of Homeland Security (DHS)
Environmental Protection Agency (EPA)
National Aeronautics and Space Administration (NASA)
National Archives and Records Administration (NARA)
National Reconnaissance Office (NRO)
National Science Foundation (NSF)

Office of Management and Budget (OMB)
Office of Science and Technology Policy (OSTP)
National Coordination Office for
Networking and Information Technology Research and Development (NITRD/NCO)

Big Data Senior Steering Group

Co-Chairs

Chaitanya Baru
Senior Advisor for Data Science
National Science Foundation

Allen Dearry
Associate Director for Research Coordination,
Planning, and Translation
National Institute of Environmental Health Sciences
(NIEHS)
National Institutes of Health (NIH)

Members

Marc Allen
Deputy Associate Administrator for Research
Science Mission Directorate
National Aeronautical and Space Administration
(NASA)

Laura Biven
Senior Science and Technology Advisor
Office of the Deputy Director for Science Programs
Department of Energy (DOE)

Robert J. Bonneau
Office of the Assistant Secretary of Defense for
Research and Engineering
Office of the Secretary of Defense

Stephen Dennis
Program Manager
Science and Technology Directorate
Department of Homeland Security (DHS)

Alan Hall
CLASS Operations Manager/ Enterprise Architect
National Oceanic and Atmospheric Administration
(NOAA)

Thuc Hoang
Program Manager
Office of Advanced Simulation and Computing
National Nuclear Security Administration (NNSA)
Department of Energy (DOE)

Suzanne Iacono
Acting Office Head
Office of Integrative Activities (OIA)
National Science Foundation (NSF)

Staff

Wendy Wigen
Technical Coordinator, Big Data Senior Steering
Group
National Coordination Office for Networking and
Information Technology Research and Development

James Keiser
Technical Director, Laboratory for Analytic Sciences
National Security Agency (NSA)

John Launchbury
Office Director
Information Innovation Office
Defense Advanced Research Projects Agency
(DARPA)

James St. Pierre
Deputy Director
Information Technology Laboratory
National Institute of Standards and Technology
(NIST)

James Szykman
Environmental Engineer
Environmental Sciences Division
Environmental Protection Agency (EPA)

Participants

Sky Bristol
Applied Earth Systems Informatics Research
Manager
United States Geological Survey (USGS)
Department of the Interior (DOI)

Mark Peterson
Division Chief for Data and Analytics
United States Agency for International Development
(USAID)

May 19, 2016

Dear Colleagues:

We are pleased to present *The Federal Big Data Research and Development Strategic Plan* of the National Science and Technology Council (NSTC). The Plan stems from activities started under the Big Data Research and Development (R&D) Initiative that the Administration launched in 2012 to harness benefits from the many rich sources of Big Data. Because of progress made under the Big Data R&D Initiative, a Big Data innovation ecosystem is emerging among Federal agencies, and leading to enhanced knowledge discovery and more confident decision-making.

The Big Data R&D Strategic Plan provides a shared vision of the R&D that will drive applications that directly benefit society and the economy of the Nation. The Plan was developed by the Big Data Senior Steering Group (BD SSG), an interagency group under the Networking and Information Technology Research and Development (NITRD) Program, based on inputs from a series of meetings, workshops, events, and activities. The Plan provides guidance on strategies for Federal agencies to use when developing, or expanding, their individual Big Data R&D plans. In the early days of its development, the BD SSG member agencies agreed unanimously that the Plan should include Big Data R&D strategies that are important regardless of scientific domain or agency mission. They further agreed that each agency should use the Plan in its own way, shaped by the agency's mission, resources, and constraints. Roadmaps, timelines, or suggestions for prioritizing different projects, therefore, are not provided: these next steps are left to individual agencies. The BD SSG will continue to help promulgate the strategies and decide which candidate topics are appropriate for Federal agency collaboration.

We look forward to continuing this important work with Federal agencies and other key partners and using this Plan to guide future decisions in Big Data research and development.

Sincerely,

James F. Kurose
Assistant Director, Computer
and Information Science and Engineering
Directorate, National Science Foundation

Keith A. Marzullo
Director, National Coordination Office for
Networking and Information Technology
Research and Development

Co-Chairs, Subcommittee on Networking and Information Technology Research and Development

Contents

Executive Summary

A national Big Data[1] innovation ecosystem is essential to enabling knowledge discovery from and confident action informed by the vast resource of new and diverse datasets that are rapidly becoming available in nearly every aspect of life. Big Data has the potential to radically improve the lives of all Americans. It is now possible to combine disparate, dynamic, and distributed datasets and enable everything from predicting the future behavior of complex systems to precise medical treatments, smart energy usage, and focused educational curricula. Government agency research and public-private partnerships, together with the education and training of future data scientists, will enable applications that directly benefit society and the economy of the Nation.

To derive the greatest benefits from the many, rich sources of Big Data, the Administration announced a "Big Data Research and Development Initiative" on March 29, 2012.[2] Dr. John P. Holdren, Assistant to the President for Science and Technology and Director of the Office of Science and Technology Policy, stated that the initiative "promises to transform our ability to use Big Data for scientific discovery, environmental and biomedical research, education, and national security."

The Federal Big Data Research and Development Strategic Plan (Plan) builds upon the promise and excitement of the myriad applications enabled by Big Data with the objective of guiding Federal agencies as they develop and expand their individual mission-driven programs and investments related to Big Data. The Plan is based on inputs from a series of Federal agency and public activities, and a shared vision:

> *We envision a Big Data innovation ecosystem in which the ability to analyze, extract information from, and make decisions and discoveries based upon large, diverse, and real-time datasets enables new capabilities for Federal agencies and the Nation at large; accelerates the process of scientific discovery and innovation; leads to new fields of research and new areas of inquiry that would otherwise be impossible; educates the next generation of 21st century scientists and engineers; and promotes new economic growth.[3]*

The Plan is built around seven strategies that represent key areas of importance for Big Data research and development (R&D). Priorities listed within each strategy highlight the intended outcomes that can be addressed by the missions and research funding of NITRD agencies. These include advancing human understanding in all branches of science, medicine, and security; ensuring the Nation's continued leadership in research and development; and enhancing the Nation's ability to address pressing societal and environmental issues facing the Nation and the world through research and development.

Strategy 1: Create next-generation capabilities by leveraging emerging Big Data foundations, techniques, and technologies. Continued, increasing investments in the next generation of large-scale data collection, management, and analysis will allow agencies to adapt to and manage the ever-increasing scales of data being generated, and leverage the data to create fundamentally new services and capabilities. Advances in computing and data analytics will provide new abstractions to deal with complex data, and simplify programming of scalable and parallel systems while achieving maximal performance. Fundamental advances in computer science, machine learning, and statistics will enable future data-analytics systems that are flexible, responsive, and predictive. Innovations in deep learning will be needed to create knowledge bases of interconnected information from unstructured data. Research into social computing such as crowdsourcing, citizen science, and collective distributed tasks will help develop techniques to enable humans to mediate tasks that may be beyond the scope of computers. New techniques and methods for interacting with and visualizing data will enhance the "human-data" interface.

Strategy 2: Support R&D to explore and understand trustworthiness of data and resulting knowledge, to make better decisions, enable breakthrough discoveries, and take confident action. To ensure the trustworthiness of information and knowledge derived from Big Data, appropriate methods and quantification approaches are needed to capture uncertainty in data as well as to ensure reproducibility and replicability of results. This is especially important when data is repurposed for a use different than the one for which the data was originally collected, and when data is integrated from multiple, heterogeneous sources of different quality. Techniques and tools are needed to promote transparency in data-driven decision making, including tools that provide detailed audits of the decision-making process to show, for example, the steps that led to a specific action. Research is needed on metadata frameworks to support trustworthiness of data, including recording the context and semantics of the data, which may evolve over time. Interpreting the results from analyses to decide upon appropriate courses of action may require human involvement. Interdisciplinary research is needed in the use of machine learning in data-driven decision making and discovery systems to examine how data can be used to best support and enhance human judgment.

Strategy 3: Build and enhance research cyberinfrastructure that enables Big Data innovation in support of agency missions. Investment in advanced research cyberinfrastructure is essential in order to keep pace with the growth in data, stay globally competitive in cutting-edge scientific research, and fulfill agency missions. A coordinated national strategy is needed to identify the needs and requirements for secure, advanced cyberinfrastructure to support handling and analyzing the vast amounts of data, including large numbers of real-time data streams from the Internet of Things (IoT), available for applications in commerce, science, defense, and other areas with Federal agency involvement—all while preserving and protecting individual privacy. Shared benchmarks, standards, and metrics will be essential for a well-functioning cyberinfrastructure ecosystem. Participatory design is necessary to optimize the usefulness and minimize the consequences of the infrastructure for all stakeholders. Education and training to build human capacity is also critical: users must be properly educated and trained to fully utilize the tools available to them.

Strategy 4: Increase the value of data through policies that promote sharing and management of data. More data must be made available and accessible on a sustained basis to maximize value and impact. The scale and heterogeneity of Big Data present significant challenges in data sharing. Encouraging data sharing, including sharing of source data, interfaces, metadata, and standards, and encouraging interoperability of associated infrastructure, improves the accessibility and value of existing data, and enhances the ability to perform new analyses on combined datasets. Building upon the current state of best practices and standards for data sharing, as well as developing new technologies to improve discoverability, usability, and transferability for data sharing, will enable more effective use of resources for future development. Research is necessary at the "human-data" interface to support the development of flexible, efficient, and usable data interfaces to fit the specific needs of different user groups. Federal agencies that provide R&D funding can assist through policies to incentivize the Big Data and data science research communities to provide comprehensive documentation on their analysis workflows and related data, driven by metadata standards and annotation systems. Such efforts will encourage greater data reuse and provide a greater return on research investments.

Strategy 5: Understand Big Data collection, sharing, and use with regard to privacy, security, and ethics. Privacy, security, and ethical concerns are key considerations in the Big Data innovation ecosystem. Privacy concerns affect how information is viewed and managed by data collectors and data providers; security concerns about personal information demand attention to data protection; and ethical concerns about the possibilities of data analyses leading to discriminatory practices have reignited civil rights debates. Research in Big Data is necessary to understand and address the variety of needs and demands of different application domains to achieve practical solutions to challenges in data privacy, security, and ethics. New policy solutions may be necessary to protect privacy and clarify data ownership. Techniques and tools are needed to help assess data security, and to secure data, in the highly distributed networks that are becoming increasingly common in Big Data application scenarios. The ability to perform comprehensive evaluations of data lifecycles is necessary to determine the long-term risk of retaining, or removing datasets. Additionally, the Nation must promote ethics in Big Data by ensuring that technologies do not propagate errors or disadvantage certain groups, either explicitly or implicitly. Efforts to explore ethics-sensitive Big Data research would enable stakeholders to better consider values and societal ethics of Big Data innovation alongside utility, risk, and cost.

Strategy 6: Improve the national landscape for Big Data education and training to fulfill increasing demand for both deep analytical talent and analytical capacity for the broader workforce. A comprehensive education strategy is essential to meet increasing workforce demands in Big Data and ensure that the United States remains economically competitive. Efforts are needed to determine the core educational requirements of data scientists, and investments are needed to support the next generation of data scientists and increase the number of data-science faculty and researchers. As scientific research becomes richer in data, domain scientists need access to opportunities to further their data-science skills, including projects that foster collaborations with data scientists, data-science short courses, and initiatives to supplement training through seed grants, professional-development stipends, and fellowships. In addition, employees and managers in all sectors need access to training "boot camps," professional-development workshops, and certificate programs to learn the relevance of Big Data to their organizations. More university courses on foundational topics and other short-term training modules are also necessary to help transform the broader workforce into data-enabled citizens. Data-science training should extend to all people through online courses, citizen-science projects, and K-12 education. Research in data-science education should explore the notion of data literacy, curricular models for providing data literacy, and the data-science skills to be taught at various grade levels.

Strategy 7: Create and enhance connections in the national Big Data innovation ecosystem. Persistent mechanisms should be established to increase the ability of agencies to partner in Big Data R&D both by removing the bureaucratic hurdles for technology and data sharing and by building sustainable programs. One such possible mechanism is the creation of cross-agency development sandboxes or testbeds to help agencies collaborate on new technologies and convert R&D output into innovative and useful capabilities. Another is the development of policies to allow for rapid and dynamic sharing of data across agency boundaries in response to urgent priorities, such as national disasters. A third is the formation of Big Data "benchmarking centers" that focus on grand challenge applications and help determine the datasets, analysis tools, and interoperability requirements necessary in achieving key national priority goals. And, finally, a national Big Data innovation ecosystem needs a strong community of practitioners across Federal agencies to facilitate rapid innovation, ensure long-term propagation of ideas, and provide maximal return on research investments.

Introduction

The Federal Big Data Research and Development Strategic Plan (Plan) defines a set of interrelated strategies for Federal agencies that conduct or sponsor R&D in data sciences, data-intensive applications, and large-scale data management and analysis. These strategies support a national Big Data innovation ecosystem in which the ability to analyze, extract information from, and make decisions and discoveries based on large, diverse, and real-time datasets enables new capabilities for both Federal agencies and the Nation at large; accelerates the process of scientific discovery and innovation; leads to new fields of research and new areas of inquiry that would otherwise be impossible; educates the next generation of 21st century scientists and engineers; and promotes new economic growth.

In March 2012, the Obama Administration announced the Big Data Research and Development Initiative[4] to leverage the fast-growing volumes of digital data to help solve some of the Nation's most pressing challenges. The Initiative calls for increasing government support and R&D investment to accelerate the Federal agencies' ability to draw insights from large and complex collections of digital data. To augment Federal agency activities, the Administration reached out to other Big Data stakeholders in private industry, academia, state and local governments, and nonprofits and foundations to collaborate on new Big Data innovation projects. In November 2013, dozens of public and private organizations gathered at an event, "Data to Knowledge to Action,"[5] sponsored by the White House's OSTP and the NITRD Program. Together, public and private partners announced an inspiring array of new projects that address such national priorities as economic development, healthcare, energy sustainability, public safety, and national security.

In 2014, the NITRD Big Data Senior Steering Group (SSG) initiated a process to summarize findings and produce a coordinated Big Data R&D agenda. Through a series of internal workshops, NITRD agency representatives examined a range of game-changing ideas with the potential to drive Big Data innovations. The Big Data SSG then synthesized the body of ideas and information into a cross-agency framework. Public comment on this framework was solicited in a Request for Information and a workshop was convened at Georgetown University to engage non-government Big Data experts and stakeholders. This document is the result of these efforts.

A primary objective of this document is to outline the key Big Data R&D strategies necessary to keep the Nation competitive in data science and innovation and to prepare for the data-intensive challenges of tomorrow. As a strategic plan, this document provides guidance for Federal agencies and policymakers in determining how to direct limited resources into activities that have the greatest potential to generate the greatest impact. The Plan profiles R&D areas that span multiple disciplines, surfacing intersections of common interest that could stimulate collaboration among researchers and technical experts in government, private industry, and academia. The Plan also offers ideas for decision makers to consider when deliberating about investments in Big Data in their respective domains. Additionally, this Plan is the Big Data SSG's response to Recommendation 11c of the 2015 review of NITRD by the President's Council of Advisors on Science and Technology (PCAST)[6] to "coordinate a process to publish and publicly discuss periodically a research and coordination plan for its area of interest."

The Plan is built around the following seven strategies that represent key areas of importance for Big Data research and development (R&D):

- Strategy 1: Create next-generation capabilities by leveraging emerging Big Data foundations, techniques, and technologies.

- Strategy 2: Support R&D to explore and understand trustworthiness of data and resulting knowledge, to make better decisions, enable breakthrough discoveries, and take confident action.

- Strategy 3: Build and enhance research cyberinfrastructure that enables Big Data innovation in support of agency missions.

- Strategy 4: Increase the value of data through policies that promote sharing and management of data.

- Strategy 5: Understand Big Data collection, sharing, and use with regard to privacy, security, and ethics.

- Strategy 6: Improve the national landscape for Big Data education and training to fulfill increasing demand for both deep analytical talent and analytical capacity for the broader workforce.

- Strategy 7: Create and enhance connections in the national Big Data innovation ecosystem.

Strategies

Strategy 1: *Create next-generation capabilities by leveraging emerging Big Data foundations, techniques, and technologies*

As Big Data technologies mature, society will increasingly rely on data-driven science to lead to new discoveries and data-driven decision making as the basis of confident action. To address new challenges in Big Data, there should be continuous and increasing investments in research on technologies for large-scale data collection, management, analysis, and the conversion of data-to-knowledge-to-action; and on the privacy, security, and ethical issues of Big Data. In the past, Federal investments in foundational research in computer science—encompassing topics ranging from computer architecture and networking technologies to algorithms, data management, artificial intelligence, machine learning, and development and deployment of advanced cyberinfrastructure—have served as major drivers of the Nation's successes in scientific discovery, Internet commerce, and national security. R&D investments by NITRD agencies resulted in the creation of the Internet that in turn enables today's generation of Big Data. NITRD agency-funded research in algorithms, such as *PageRank*[7] and *FastBit*,[8] resulted in the creation of robust indexing and search engine capabilities. Most recently, the discovery of the Higgs boson was enabled by the development of algorithms to identify complex signals from petabytes of data.[9]

Scale Up to Keep Pace with the Size, Speed, and Complexity of Data

Big Data encompasses a range of data scenarios—from large and rapid data streams to highly distributed and heterogeneous data-collection networks. Big Data contexts may require high-performance and complex processing of data, and very large warehouses and archives for data storage. As highlighted by the National Strategic Computing Initiative,[10] there is a need to scale up computing systems to deal with the sizes, rates, and extreme syntactic (format) as well as semantic (meaning) heterogeneity of such data. Further, for human users, the overall system must provide highly interactive, easy-to-use interfaces to allow human users to be "in the loop" to control the system, as well as to use the information and knowledge products generated by it.

Many NITRD agencies are tasked with the development and maintenance of major scientific experiments, observations, and simulations that generate unprecedented volumes of data. Scientists increasingly want to integrate these datasets to facilitate discovery. Dedicated networks are needed to transport large volumes of scientific data generated at experimental facilities (such as the Large Hadron Collider at CERN or the new Linac Coherent Light Source at SLAC National Accelerator Laboratory) to distant and, in some cases, distributed computing resources for analysis. Data-management bottlenecks can occur at almost every stage of the scientific workflow including capturing data from an experimental or computing facility, transporting it for further analysis, and analyzing and visualizing the data, as well as finding appropriate environments for sharing data.

A range of computer system architectures are required to serve the wide range of applications requirements—from tightly interconnected systems to more loosely coupled, distributed systems. Large system configurations, high-speed network interconnects, deep memory hierarchies, and high performance storage systems will be required in order to process large-scale and high-speed data interactively. These systems must be resilient and autonomic to deal with hardware and software faults and failures. New abstractions will be necessary to simplify the challenges of programming such systems and exploiting parallelism for scheduling computation, communication, and output for interactive as well as batch-oriented Big Data applications. The proper set of abstractions must be provided to enable applications to specify their resource requirements and execute efficiently in an environment with shared resources.

Naive scaling of current tools and techniques will not be sufficient as Big Data applications confront and supersede hard limits in, for example, input/output data rates from computing systems, or the amount of data that a human can perceive or understand, even using visualization. Biases may need to be introduced for the sake of tractability, requiring fundamentally new techniques and understanding.

Along with convergence in architectural approaches, there are opportunities for coordination and collaborations between computational science (the Third Paradigm) and data science (the Fourth Paradigm). In many scenarios, complex computational models are validated via evaluation-driven research programs where Big Data is collected and analytics are measured in experimental settings. Conversely, many Big Data problems lead, eventually, to the creation and execution of computational models. Many techniques, tools, and approaches can be shared between both communities, especially if investments in measurement science yield metrics and evaluation frameworks that are generalizable across the many challenges that exist between computational and data science. What emerges is a fundamentally new workflow for scientific discovery where simulation and experimental data are inextricably linked. Advances in computation and data analysis need to be coordinated.[11]

Big Data application scenarios are typically characterized by large-scale system configurations—for example, within a datacenter, across widely distributed datacenters, or across the IoT. With rapid changes in hardware and software technologies, and evolving applications needs and requirements, the notion of Software Defined Environments (SDE) or Software Defined Infrastructure (SDI) becomes important within the context of such large configurations. Different types of applications, or different phases within a given application, may require different configurations among various system components. In many cases, Big Data applications may execute within a cloud environment where the cloud provider provides a generic system that can be customized for a particular computation using SDE. In other scenarios, when the cost of moving data is too high and latencies become a major roadblock, future infrastructures may help move the computation to the data. National platforms, such as the Global Environment for Network Innovations (GENI)[12] must continue to provide the large-scale experimental testbeds to carry out such research. In addition, public-private, national-state level partnerships, such as US Ignite,[13] are necessary to foster novel applications and digital experiences.

Big Data applications must deal with data from multiple sources that may be heterogeneous in a variety of ways, such as the syntax and semantics of the data, the quality of the data, and the policy regime under which the data was produced and by which it can be used. Core technical infrastructure to enable representation of semantic information is a key next-generation capability for Big Data.

A core capability for enabling such applications is a semantic information infrastructure to enable easier discovery of relevant data and integration across related datasets. Scalable approaches are needed to tackle the full scope of this problem. Techniques employed can range from automated machine-learning algorithms to human-in-the-loop approaches, including crowdsourcing methods. One of the critical technology components is named entity identification, to assist in transforming unstructured data to structured data. New directions for research are opening up in this area as well as in data quality, which is being explored by a number of agencies.

DHS Homeland Security Advanced Research Projects Agency (HSARPA)

CONNECTED, PROTECTED, AND FULLY AWARE

Image courtesy of the Homeland Security Advanced Research Projects Agency.

Thick smoke, scorching heat, and blaring alarm bells fill the building. Over 60 pounds of protective gear and countless hours of training help support our Nation's firefighters, but timely and accurate situational awareness or "scene size-up" remains a challenge on every call.

The Department of Homeland Security (DHS) operates the National Fire Incident Report System (NFIRS) to gather and analyze information on the Nation's fires. Despite today's education, research, and training efforts, fires kill over 3,000 people and injure over 17,000 people nationwide each year. Annual property loss due to fire approaches $12 billion. Most of these fatalities, injuries, and losses are preventable.

In partnership with the Federal Emergency Management Agency (FEMA) and the US Fire Administration (USFA), HSARPA developed an analytical prototype and worked with four regional fire departments to explore ~225 million NFIRS incidents at the national, state, and regional levels. Big Data technologies such as geospatial and graph analytics were used to identify trends and patterns about incident types, equipment failures, and firefighter casualties, delivering new insights on how to improve training and reduce losses.

The IoT is a rapidly emerging source of Big Data. Estimates are that by 2018 over half of Internet traffic will originate not from computers but from devices.[14] The devices in this category include sensors of all types, mobile phones, and other consumer and industrial electronic devices. Increasingly, instrumented systems or environments are becoming the norm in science and engineering scenarios. Federal agency-funded scientific research is pioneering new approaches, such as the National Ecological Observatory Network (NEON),[15] that are deploying large numbers of heterogeneous sensors and sensor networks that will collect large amounts of heterogeneous data. New tools are needed to unify and organize this information into human- and machine-readable summaries in a timely fashion. Many of these environments are characterized as cyber-physical systems because they seamlessly integrate computational algorithms and physical components. New technologies for handling the breadth and scope of data from IoT will be essential for many future Big Data applications.

Develop New Methods to Enable Future Big Data Capabilities

Cutting-edge data management, querying, and analysis techniques in computer science must be linked with fundamental approaches in statistics and machine learning to create data systems that are flexible, responsive, and predictive. Computer-science techniques need to incorporate more statistical approaches, while statistical techniques need to develop approaches for trading off statistical power and computational complexity. This merging of computer science and statistical techniques will usher in a "Smart Data" era with enormous opportunities for new applications. However, the scalability of statistical methods also poses a major challenge. When data becomes big, the possible number of simultaneous hypotheses, as well as data points, can be on the order of millions.[16] Robust statistical algorithms may not run within an acceptable time frame, forcing users to rely on less sophisticated and more error-prone algorithms. Integration of statistical inference principles as part of Big Data will be essential to resolve these challenges.

A suite of tools and best practices is also needed for real-time statistical inference using data streams. These tools and best practices should process data-quality information, be scalable, and be able to support a broad range of application areas, such as security, bioinformatics, consumer behavior, climate, civic infrastructure, and demographics.

A large class of new Big Data applications is required to deal with diverse sources and forms of data, ranging from highly structured to unstructured data. Data-driven model development is a key approach to extracting structure and meaning from Big Data. Machine-learning techniques are essential to this endeavor. Research is needed in deep learning methods that can add identification and predictive power to data and algorithms. The structure of the human brain, based on studies from the BRAIN Initiative,[17] may itself provide new insights and inspiration for a new generation of neural network algorithms and computing architectures, and lead to research in areas such as neuromorphic computing.

DOD Defense Advanced Research Projects Agency (DARPA)

MAKING SENSE OUT OF THE COMPLEX

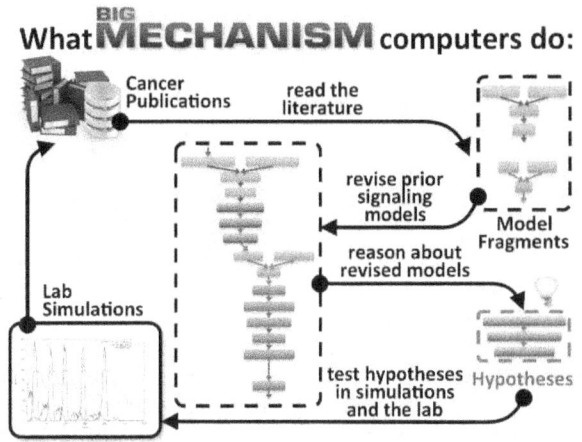

Illustration courtesy of the Defense Advanced Research Projects Agency.

Some of the systems that matter most to us are very complicated. Ecosystems, the brain, social systems, and the economy have many parts and processes. These processes, however, are often studied piecewise, and the literature and data on them can be fragmented, distributed, and inconsistent. Although the collection of Big Data is increasingly automated, the creation of big mechanisms (that is, the full explanations of complicated systems), remains a human endeavor. DARPA's Big Mechanism program aims to speed up the scientific research process by enabling machines to read, synthesize, and reason about complicated systems. The goal of the program is to develop technologies for a new kind of science in which research is integrated immediately into causal, explanatory models of unprecedented completeness and consistency.

The first challenge taken on by Big Mechanism researchers is cancer biology. The program is working on machine reading of scientific papers to identify molecular interactions in signaling pathways, modeling languages to integrate fragments of knowledge into large models, and algorithms to identify possible drug targets that show promise. Tools developed by the Big Mechanism program may enable a new kind of scholarship, in which scientists model and understand entire systems, not just system components.

While automated techniques can greatly improve productivity, humans continue to perform some tasks better, such as in data identification, curation, and categorization. Systems for human-aided computation can range from the computational tools that put scientists and experts "in the loop" to expansive platforms for crowdsourcing and citizen science. These "social computing" systems employ various methods of engagement, including social media, peer production, crowdsourcing, and collective distributed tasks. In many citizen-science projects, such as Galaxy Zoo[18] and Foldit,[19] and collaboration experiments like the DARPA Network Challenge, human volunteers provided insights and discoveries that expert analysis missed. The 2013 PCAST review of NITRD identified social computing as an area ripe for further attention and investment, particularly noting the potential of mobilizing citizens to address national priorities in health, public safety, and science.[20] Incorporating human workers (volunteer or paid) into data-processing workflows could augment analysis capabilities and benefit many applications.

DOE Advanced Scientific Computing Research program (ASCR)

INTERACTIVE EXPLORATION OF ENORMOUS DATA

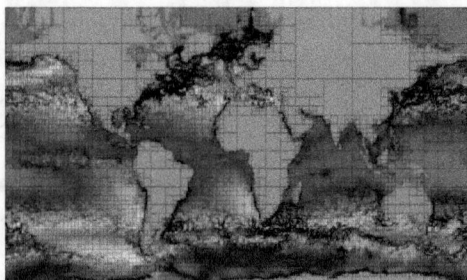

Image courtesy of Los Alamos National Laboratory.

"A picture is worth a thousand words," but how do you picture a billion data values computed by a simulation? The idea is daunting. Nevertheless, the In Situ Big Data Visualization of Scientific Climate Data project, funded by DOE ASCR, aims to understand the impact of climate change on the Nation's power infrastructure (e.g., power plants). To achieve this ambitious goal, scientists need the next generation of climate simulations and exascale supercomputers.

Current practices for analyzing simulation data rely on moving the data from the supercomputer that runs simulations to another computing environment for manipulation and analysis. In the era of exascale computing, such practices will not be feasible because of the vastly larger datasets involved and the very limited bandwidth and storage for moving and saving data. This project will use "in situ" analysis, which will allow scientists to process the data before it is moved, thereby transporting and storing only the data that provides new insights and discoveries.

The In Situ Big Data Visualization of Scientific Climate Data project brings together an in situ workflow for data reduction and a visualization tool called ParaView. The combination will allow researchers to interactively explore simulations and extract meaningful information from datasets that would otherwise be inscrutable. These new tools and techniques will help scientists visualize, analyze, and understand the potential impacts of climate on our energy production and power infrastructure over long periods of time and for specific regions. In addition, the tools and techniques are transferable to other science disciplines that face similar challenges with their data.

Given the complexity of Big Data, there are key roles for metadata, uncertainty information, and quality visualizations to play in understanding its significance. Further research and innovation is needed to detect both the expected and unexpected; provide timely, defensible, and understandable assessments; and communicate those insights effectively. This will require multi-user, multi-stakeholder engagements that are equipped with the necessary collaborative environments and tools.

Many Big Data analyses begin with discovering correlations among factors, which can provide important insights into underlying phenomena. Research and advances in measurement science are needed in hypothesis generation, causal inference, and other fundamental statistical methods using Big Data. Progress in these areas will allow researchers to obtain better insights and recognize spurious correlations, which might lead to incorrect conclusions. Robust techniques are also needed for representing and processing data quality information.

Strategy 2: *Support R&D to explore and understand trustworthiness of data and resulting knowledge, to make better decisions, enable breakthrough discoveries, and take confident action*

Traditional statistical approaches are used to handle "designed" datasets derived from controlled experiments or surveys. Big Data is often comprised of such designed data, but also may include data collected "opportunistically," or collected for one purpose and reused for another. The data may have been processed through a series of incremental analyses, each for a different purpose. These characteristics make it challenging to provide a holistic view of the data and the uncertainty in the underlying information.

This major challenge in today's Big Data landscape is due, in part, from the rise in the sharing and availability of data facilitated by the Internet and promoted by several U.S. Government policies. There is also a growing recognition among data scientists that access to relevant data is essential for building on previous results. The consequence is that data users are increasingly removed from the generators or collectors of the data they use. As the expectation for data access grows, data users will need to understand and assess how data can be used and whether the source is trustworthy. However, deriving accurate knowledge from data puts burdens on both the data disseminator and the data user. Data that is appropriately documented, formatted, and accompanied by complete and meaningful metadata facilitates confident use. Robust measures are needed to quantify uncertainty and capture context to ensure reproducibility of results; this will give decision makers the ability to validate the trustworthiness of the data and the products of analyses. Decision makers will require tools for parsing the relevant knowledge applicable to decisions, converting knowledge into possible action, and understanding the implications and impact of those actions.

Understand the Trustworthiness of Data and Validity of Knowledge

In the Information Quality Act of 2001, the White House Office of Management and Budget (OMB) recognized the importance of the quality of data disseminated by Federal agencies.[21] In general, determining overall "trustworthiness" of data is a challenging task—the definition of the term may vary depending upon the application scenario and use-case. In one framework employed in the social sciences,[22] trustworthiness is delineated into the truthfulness (i.e., internal validity or credibility), applicability (i.e., external validity or transferability), consistency (i.e., reliability or dependability), and neutrality (i.e., objectivity or confirmability) of the information. Inferences based on data would need to account for which of the characteristics are satisfied by the data.

The scale, heterogeneity, and rapidly changing nature of Big Data further complicate the notions of trustworthiness and inference. Traditional tests for validity, soundness, and significance may need to be modified and adapted. Quantities such as accuracy, error, precision, anomalies, authenticity, and uncertainty may need to be measured and tracked to enable robust data-driven decision making. Software may be required to track the propagation of these quantities through multi-step and iterative processing pipelines, complex transformations, and integration across heterogeneous data sources.

Understanding data trustworthiness is essential in order to derive accurate inferences from Big Data. Research is needed to develop robust statistical techniques that use a wide diversity of data inputs. Interdisciplinary research is also needed to create state-of-the-art techniques that combine heuristics (trial and error) and statistics. A key differentiator of Big Data is the *ex post facto* discovery of uses for previously collected data. Another is the combining of independently collected datasets, each of which may fulfill different assumptions. Interpreting the output quality of statistical tests on this type of data depends upon the specific type of statistical test being performed, i.e., the nature of the question being asked, which may vary by application. Traditional statistical tests may be insufficient. New, innovative techniques may be needed for Big Data.

In data science, replicability is the ability to rerun the exact data experiment—with the same data inputs, parameter settings, and computations—to produce exactly the same result. Reproducibility is the ability to use different data, techniques, and/or equipment to confirm the same result as previously obtained. Both are fundamental to the validations of results and conclusions drawn from data. NITRD agencies are interested in replicability and reproducibility for science R&D applications as well as for decision-making applications. However, both are challenging notions to implement in a Big Data computing environment, where datasets can be extremely large and constantly evolving. Both a common framework and a common understanding of these concepts are needed to help improve the trustworthiness of data and computed results.

NIST Information Technology Laboratory (ITL) and Materials Measurement Laboratory (MML)

BATTLING VISION LOSS IN AMERICA

Slowly going blind is the challenge faced by over 7 million Americans with age-related macular degeneration (AMD). AMD is the leading cause of blindness in adults, but effective treatments, such as cell-based therapies, could offer a way to replace damaged eye tissue with healthy tissue and save the Nation $30 billion annually in lost GDP. However, to ensure the effectiveness of cell-based therapies, decisions on whether to implant tissues into the patient must be made based on trustworthy tissue images. Big Image Data, a joint ITL and MML project, addresses the need for high quality imaging measurements with a goal of achieving 10 times the quality of current medical image interpretation. This improvement will enable individuals with AMD to be diagnosed and to receive cell-based therapies with lower risks of adverse events.

At the National Institute of Standards and Technology (NIST), the long-term goal is to provide validated methods for automated manufacturing and product release tests that will speed and improve the decision-making process. For example, the technologies developed within NIST can be reused in other fields such as materials reliability to promote trustworthy measurements.

Data processing is typically performed via analysis pipelines. Comprehensive tools and best practices are needed to ensure that existing analysis pipelines can persist into the future, and that the results can be replicated at some future point in time. The use of open-source software, data, and Application Programming Interfaces (APIs) can be key enablers in this regard. This requires contextual information, well-defined metadata frameworks, and the ability to instantiate a past processing environment in the future. Tools such as the Code, Data, and Environment (CDE) package are able to overcome technical barriers to reproducibility by converting all software dependencies to a code that can be executed on Linux computers, other than the original Linux system. Containers, virtual machines, and packaging systems like CDE are useful tools for enabling replicability in Big Data, but these systems will need to evolve as technologies and analysis capabilities progress.

Researchers can be incentivized to adopt good practices by requiring reproducible research strategies as part of their research activity. This ensures the reliability of their analyses and allows other researchers to derive further value from past datasets and analyses. For example, the NIH's "Principles and Guidelines for Reporting Preclinical Research"[23] is a prime example of guidance that agencies can provide to improve reproducibility within a specific domain.

In addition to creating better metadata standards for future data collection, some Federal agencies must also maintain legacy scientific data whose use is limited because it lacks metadata. Agencies such as NASA are investing in technology for "data archeology" that strives to automate the generation of metadata from data content.

Learning and using proper methods and protocols for data collection, analysis, and interpretation are an essential starting point for data trustworthiness. This requires a well-educated workforce that can stay current through on-going training programs as techniques and tools evolve. This is particularly important in the Big Data world, where data and information may have diverse origins and unpredictable use. Education and training in the authoring and use of metadata and, as mentioned in the next section, adoption of strong metadata standards, will be essential.

NIH Center for Expanded Data Annotation and Retrieval (CEDAR)
ESTABLISHING BETTER DATA FOR BETTER SCIENCE

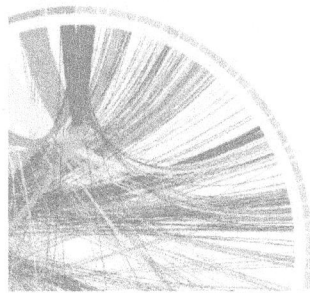

Imagine a library with an incomplete catalog that made it impossible to know where a resource might be located, what language it is written in, or whether it is a video or a document. Similar to a library's indexing methods, metadata is needed to index large numbers of experimental datasets so that they can be retrieved, reused, and properly attributed. The challenge is that creating accurate and adequate metadata is a tedious process.

Image courtesy of the Human Immunology Project Consortium.

The Center for Expanded Data Annotation and Retrieval (CEDAR) at Stanford University, funded through the NIH, wants to help investigators in the sciences achieve the promise of Big Data by making the process of metadata creation as painless as possible. CEDAR's goal is to create a unified framework that all scientific disciplines can use to create consistent, easily searchable metadata that allows researchers to locate the datasets that they need, consolidate datasets in one location, integrate multiple datasets, and reproduce the results. For example, CEDAR projects like the Human Immunology Project Consortium (HIPC) will enable widespread, free sharing of immunology data. This knowledge base will serve as a foundation for the future study of a variety of inflammatory diseases as well as immune-mediated diseases, such as allergy, asthma, transplant rejection, and autoimmune diseases.

Significant efforts are needed to curate datasets—to record the context as well as semantics associated with the data, and with the analyses performed on the data. Effective and proper reuse of data demands that the data context be properly registered and that data semantics be extracted and represented. While automation will be essential to accomplish this for Big Data, tasks related to curation, context, and semantics will also require a human-in-the-loop approach. Tools and ecosystems are needed to assist in this task, such as entity identification that utilizes global persistent identifiers and the use of domain ontologies for knowledge representation. Research in metadata modeling, automated metadata generation and registration, semantic technologies, ontologies, linked data, data provenance, and data citation will be important.

Some metadata may change or evolve over time, depending on how the data is used, the presence of new datasets, etc. Ontologies may also evolve with the addition of new data and information. While well-defined metadata frameworks are essential for capturing this information, research will also need to take into account the evolution of such information over time. Tools may be needed to bridge data collections by retrofitting and migrating older metadata into schemas compatible with current and future collection efforts.

Design Tools to Support Data-Driven Decision-Making

From algorithmic stock trading to managing the smart electric grid, systems used today are increasingly automated. However, the vast majority of data-driven decision-making systems still require human intervention. In almost all complex decisions, humans must interpret the information generated from algorithms, determine the validity of the information in the given context, take policy considerations into account, and then decide upon an appropriate course of action. Research is needed on how technology can best augment human judgment in such data-driven decision-making scenarios, in order to better inform their choices as well as increase the speed at which trustworthy and confident decisions and actions can be taken.

The next generation of data-driven decision-making systems must also be adaptive and have the ability to integrate analysis of real-time data flows with historical data. Human-mediated decision making will remain essential in these complex, multifaceted situations, where information may be derived from multiple heterogeneous sources. User-friendly interfaces to these complex decision support systems and environments will be needed.

Another key requirement is to establish the provenance of data-driven decisions, with tools to make the decision-making process reproducible, traceable, and transparent. In order to build trust in data-driven systems, the tools must clearly and succinctly enumerate the steps by which conclusions were reached.

Machine-learning approaches, including deep learning systems, are also needed to build better data-driven models that can be used to reliably augment human decision making. Artificial Intelligence (AI) research will have profound impacts on decision-making systems. Question and answer systems that automate answers to human-posed questions (e.g., IBM's Watson), and systems that reason (e.g., DARPA's Big Mechanism program) are examples of how AI can augment human capabilities. These systems are a resource for human decision makers, who can now leverage a much broader knowledge base as input while minimizing human biases in their output. Big Data SSG agencies recognize that research into the foundational areas of AI is critical to creating systems that make Big Data more actionable.

Given the complexity of information that will be available in the future, decision-support systems must also be capable of functioning in a collaborative manner with multiple agents to satisfy multiple objectives. Humans are often asked to make decisions that satisfy a disparate and potentially divergent set of end goals. Intelligent agents must be capable of operating under similar circumstances. A decision-making system must be able to either reconcile these criteria within a recommended course of action or present clear options and consequences that allow a human to understand and decide, while also taking into account high-level policy considerations.

National Science Foundation (NSF) and the Treasury Office of Financial Research (OFR)

SHINE A LIGHT INTO DARK CORNERS

The 2007-2009 financial crisis made clear that our understanding of the financial system was deficient in many respects. Market participants and regulators underestimated how disruptions could emerge and spread quickly across interconnected companies and markets, with severe consequences for the economy. As a result, in 2010, Congress created the Office of Financial Research (OFR) to serve the needs of the Financial Stability Oversight Council and its member agencies. OFR's mission is to shine a light in the dark corners of the financial system to see where risks are going, assess how much of a threat they might pose, and provide policymakers with the information, the policy tools, and the analysis to mitigate them.

The OFR is a virtual research-and-data community that uses a collaborative approach to expand its capacity to meet urgent needs and complement the work of others in the financial sector. To accomplish its goals, the OFR has partnered with the National Science Foundation to support Big Data financial-stability research, policymaking, and decision-making. This program involves collaboration by computer scientists, statisticians, economists, social scientists, and financial experts in using Big Data tools and techniques to identify and assess risks to the financial stability of the United States. The research will help support a more transparent, efficient, and stable financial system.

To ensure trustworthy, robust conclusions and decisions, it is necessary to fully understand the human as well as the technical components of a data-driven decision-making system. Research in augmenting human decision making with data-driven decisions is inherently socio-technical and interdisciplinary in nature. Understanding the nature of human behavior and cognitive biases when faced with different kinds of information is as critical as the validity of the information itself. Counterintuitively, presenting more data to a human can sometimes lead to a greater chance of erroneous conclusions. For example, studies have demonstrated that when presented with gender information, clinicians tend to under-diagnose heart disease in women, as compared to men exhibiting the same symptoms.[24]

It is likely that an increasing number of decisions in the future will be mediated through Big Data knowledge processes. Decisions made by people in all walks of life will be informed by knowledge derived from Big Data. Clear communication of how that knowledge was created, and the set of robust conclusions that could be drawn from that knowledge, is valuable to experts and non-experts alike. Increased data literacy of Big Data technologies is critical to increasing the adoption of such tools and strengthening the entire "data-to-knowledge-to-action" process.

> ### *Strategy 3*: *Build and enhance research cyberinfrastructure that enables Big Data innovation in support of agency missions*

State-of-the-art cyberinfrastructure is necessary if Federal agencies are to take advantage of the opportunities that Big Data offers. Innovative advanced cyberinfrastructure will need to combine the powers of Big Data and large-scale computing into a coherent capability for data analysis;[25] address the challenges of data transport at all scales, from on the chip to across the globe;[26] and satisfy the growing need for new environments for data sharing and analytics.[27] Federal agencies have had a long history of supporting research on leading-edge infrastructure from the development of ARPANET in 1969, to the NSFNET and DOE ESnet programs, to the current NSF Global Environment for Network Innovations (GENI) program in computer networking and Extreme Digital (XD) program in high-performance computing.

Advancements in research cyberinfrastructure must serve a wide range of Big Data application needs and requirements. At the high end of computing and data, the National Strategic Computing Initiative (NSCI) provides guidance for "accelerating delivery of a capable exascale computing system that integrates hardware and software capability to deliver approximately 100 times the performance of current 10 petaflop systems across a range of applications representing government needs," with "increasing coherence between the technology base used for modeling and simulation and that used for data analytic computing." The NSCI is a "whole-of-government effort designed to create a cohesive, multi-agency strategic vision and Federal investment strategy, executed in collaboration with industry and academia, to maximize the benefits of [high-performance computing] (HPC) for the United States."[28]

In other areas of Big Data, the applications may require very different types of cyberinfrastructure. Examples include highly networked systems, such as the IoT, that may not require exascale computing, but may pose challenges to operating in a highly distributed, parallel system on data stored across deep storage/memory hierarchies, or large memory systems for in-memory operations on extremely large data structure, such as complex graphs. In concert with the NSCI and other related initiatives and activities, a coordinated national strategy is needed to identify the needs and requirements for secure, advanced cyberinfrastructure to support handling and analyzing large amounts of data. Design considerations must include the full range of data scenarios, from large-scale warehoused historical data to data from multiple, concurrent, real-time data streams. Regardless of the type of application, state-of-the-art cyberinfrastructure is essential in a data-driven world, for maintaining global competitiveness in cutting-edge scientific research, promoting a vibrant data-driven industry sector, and fulfilling the public mission of government agencies.

Strengthen the National Data Infrastructure

Datasets themselves constitute essential infrastructure for Big Data. A key aspect of the Big Data strategy is enabling access to open data, supporting sustained access, and providing controlled access to protected data. In the 1970s, research infrastructures like ARPANET and NSFNET led to the creation of the Internet. In the 1980s, a concerted effort in high-performance computing led to the creation of supercomputer centers at multiple NITRD agencies and research institutions. Today, the need is to significantly enhance national data infrastructure to exploit the full power of Big Data. While there are community-based efforts, such as the Research Data Alliance (RDA) and the National Data System (NDS), that focus on issues related to creating a national (and international) capability, the Big Data SSG is interested in a coordinated plan for a national data infrastructure that can serve the needs of a wide range of stakeholders.

There is a need to standardize access to data resources within and across agencies. The collaborative development of standards and metrics for the entire data-driven cyberinfrastructure pipeline, including the hardware, analytics, data resources, and interfaces with which they interact, will be critical for a well-functioning cyberinfrastructure ecosystem. Several agencies have highlighted the importance of developing data and metadata standards in order to improve interoperability among data resources across organizations (e.g., the NIST ISO/IEC JTC 1 Study Group on Big Data,[29] USGS Modular Science Framework[30]). An open systems approach and a federated implementation would greatly enhance the ability to share and combine datasets within and among agencies and with the public.[31] Data curation and data elements registration, development of standards, and data sharing and data integration approaches, should involve all relevant stakeholders. The approach should be federated, modular, and extensible in order to allow for agency-specific additions and enhancements. Community-based organizations such as the RDA are engaged in grassroots activities to further the development and adoption of such standards. New standards are also needed for measuring the performance and effectiveness, including price/performance, of Big Data systems. These standards should reflect end-to-end performance for realistic application scenarios, necessarily combining data-intensive and compute-intensive aspects. Initiatives under way include the NSF's Benchmarks of Realistic Scientific Application Performance of Large-Scale Computing Systems (BRAP) program[32] and the community effort to develop the Big Data Top 100 List.[33] Along with performance, the new metrics should incorporate price/performance and energy performance.

A multiplicity of solutions such as shared repositories, federated and virtual approaches, and discoverability systems are needed to share data across disciplines and among agencies. In any field, discovery is enabled by the availability of cyberinfrastructure oriented to Big Data. All Federal agencies with annual research budgets greater than $100 million have developed public access plans to increase access to the results of Federally funded scientific research, including data. DARPA supports the DARPA Open Catalog, which contains a curated list of DARPA-sponsored software and peer-reviewed publications. Many agencies support community data repositories across a wide range of science and engineering disciplines. In many fields, including those represented by the Precision Medicine Initiative and the Materials Genome Initiative, a transition is taking place from the generation of small disparate datasets (the so-called "long-tail data") to the bundling and integration of these data to enable easier discovery, access, and analysis. Programs such as the NIH BD2K and NSF's Building Community and Capacity in Data-Intensive Research in Education (BCC-EHR)[34] are vital for ensuring that all communities have access to new resources and analytical techniques to advance their fundamental research.

With advances in simulation methodologies and computing power, the validity of results from simulations could equal those from instrumentation. There will be increasing opportunities for integrating simulation data with observational and experimental data, resulting in accelerated progress of data-intensive computational research. The Big Data SSG recognizes the opportunity for a strategic effort in this area for systems and standards that enable easy sharing and use of research, government, and other open data.

Empower Advanced Scientific Cyberinfrastructure for Big Data

Investment in shared leadership high-performance computing (HPC) resources have been made by Big Data SSG agencies such as NSF and DOE, which have traditionally focused on modeling and simulation applications. Increasingly, however, agencies are also sponsoring high-end HPC systems that provide processing capabilities for data analytics, and are pushing the development of computer system architectures that can efficiently support high-performance computing for both memory and compute-intensive codes and efficient data access and processing. Among the goals of the NSCI is to promote the development of exascale systems that are also capable of performing data analytics operations efficiently.

There is growing recognition that there are significant data issues common to different disciplines and application areas, even while some issues are specific to a discipline or application area. Some aspects of cyberinfrastructure for Big Data may focus on specific application domains, while others are common and shared across multiple research domains. Investments in both categories are critical for supporting the diversity of Big Data innovation. The former is important so that domains with specific and difficult Big Data challenges can be well supported with resources optimized tor those applications; and the latter so that a shared infrastructure can offer access to resources that an individual community alone would not be able to build and sustain.

DOE Office of Science (SC)
SUPPORTING COLLABORATIVE SCIENCE AROUND THE GLOBE

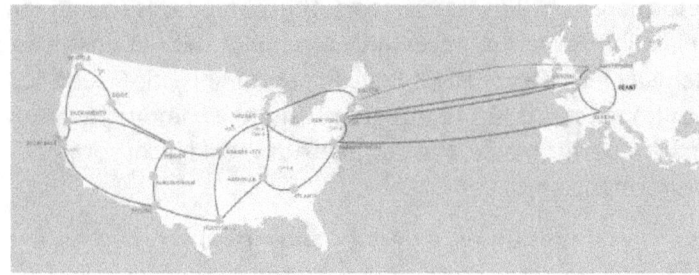

Science is global. Facilities like the Large Hadron Collider, the Advanced Light Source, and the Joint Genome Institute create multi-terabyte to multi-petabyte scale datasets that need to be disseminated and analyzed by scientists and computing

Image courtesy of the Department of Energy's Office of Science.

resources around the world. Enabling this experimentation and collaboration requires extremely fast networking speeds. The DOE Office of Science's Energy Sciences Network (ESnet) seeks to ensure that scientific progress is unconstrained by the location of experimental instruments, people, computational resources, or the size of the data. ESnet can move data at 100 gigabits per second and is engineered to be an international resource for collaborative data-intensive science.

ESnet is helping researchers with real-time feedback on experiments using DOE Office of Science light sources. For example, a detector at a light source facility can now capture data from a sample, automatically send it to a supercomputing center to be processed and visualized, and then allow the scientist to access the data from a web portal in near real time. Using ESnet, groups of scientists can get feedback on whether they have taken the right sample or if they have calibrated the experiment appropriately, thereby greatly reducing the time it takes to discover new phenomena.

There is a significant opportunity for coupling advanced cyberinfrastructure with physical data sources—whether a telescope, an MRI machine, or instrumentation at border crossings. Such a linked system could provide targeted, efficient, and effective data services and efficient pathways to appropriate computing resources. When developing this type of cyberinfrastructure, it is important to have a comprehensive understanding of the instrumentation that generates the data, have an understanding of processing and computational objectives, and collaborate with the data collection groups and end users of the data.

Address Community Needs with Flexible and Diverse Infrastructure Resources

The process of designing and developing cyberinfrastructure benefits greatly when stakeholders and the intended user-base are included. Community involvement is essential when a project requires the design of hardware that is specific to handling a particular type of data or dataset. Early stakeholder involvement optimizes the usefulness of the resulting infrastructure and minimizes unwanted consequences.

Robust cyberinfrastructure for Big Data will require real-world deployment of systems using state-of-the-art as well as emerging Big Data technologies. However, enterprise-level systems are costly and require consistent management and maintenance that may be beyond the scope of universities or mid-sized enterprises to support for testing the performance of Big Data techniques. To allow researchers to test the deployment of infrastructure that meets the current and anticipated needs of Big Data communities, there is a need to invest in cyberinfrastructure pilot programs and testbeds for specific research communities and applications that use and analyze data. Such pilot programs would provide researchers with platforms for testing new techniques at scale, across a variety of application domains. Pilot programs may include multi-site and/or multi-year projects to test collaborative infrastructure adequately. Big Data SSG agencies may need to develop new funding models or partnerships to ensure support and resources for researchers participating in pilot programs. Also, a robust transition-to-practice pipeline is an integral part of the research process to implement effective pilots.

Cloud computing provides multiple choices for implementation, including use of private clouds and public clouds. Big Data SSG agencies are already exploring multiple implementation models that are appropriate to their respective missions and organizational objectives. One example is the NIH Commons,[35] which is a shared and interoperable computing environment intended to take advantage of both private and public cloud computing platforms with HPC resources. Public clouds are increasingly used as a computing platform by biomedical researchers because they afford a high degree of scalability and flexibility in both the cost and configuration of compute services. The NIH Commons framework focuses on interoperability between resources through common container frameworks and open APIs.

The development of common tools and standards will be a critical component of a national data cyberinfrastructure. The Big Data software ecosystem is currently dominated by open-source software packages. Agencies such as the NSA have also made some of their Big Data software open source (e.g., Apache Accumulo™ and Apache NiFi™). Big Data SSG agencies have a commitment to support open-source software development that both reduces costs and produces innovative, high-quality software.

Strategy 4: Increase the value of data through policies that promote sharing and management of data

Big Data SSG agencies are dedicated to promoting a culture of data sharing and open data for government. Such a culture requires data stakeholders to play an active role in data stewardship—to mitigate losses of data and the subsequent losses of opportunities for machine learning, inference, and longitudinal studies. New policies, standards, and environments for sharing data and tools can facilitate analyses across datasets that would otherwise be impossible, thereby making new areas of research accessible. Such transformations have already occurred in fields such as biology and cosmology and are emerging in the areas of materials science and climate.

Similar to the "open-source software" movement, a robust "open-source data" movement can foster a sustainable ecosystem for discoverability, accessibility and sharing of data. Although large amounts of data are currently being generated and collected, much of it remains "dark" or inaccessible. The scale and heterogeneity of Big Data present significant new challenges that also need to be addressed. Furthermore, policies and protocols for data sharing must be created to support sustainable sharing across sectors.[36] "Data sharing" includes the curation and sharing of data itself but, equally importantly, the metadata and the APIs to the data.

Indeed, the Federal government has already been investing in data-sharing practices. There have been longstanding efforts to help catalog high-value datasets generated by agencies as well as for datasets generated within specific domains. For example, in 2009 the Chief Information Officer of the United States launched Data.gov to increase public access to all high value, machine-readable datasets created or collected by the Executive Branch of the Federal government. As a complement to Data.gov, independent agencies and interagency collaborations have also generated inventories of domain-specific datasets that use customized metadata frameworks to enable better search and discovery. For example, USAID has opened a publicly accessible Development Data Library to share data from its international development projects. The NIH National Library of Medicine catalogs over 60 different NIH Data Sharing Repositories on topics from cancer imaging to nanomaterials to drug addiction. The U.S. Group on Earth Observations (USGEO) has been working with the international Group on Earth Observations (GEO) to share high-quality data about the Earth. These datasets include information about weather systems, crops, ecosystems, etc., and come from a diverse array of scientific instruments worldwide. In addition, Federal agencies support international community-based data sharing efforts and organizations such as the Committee on Data for Science and Technology (CODATA) and the Research Data Alliance (RDA).

Develop Best Practices for Metadata to Increase Data Transparency and Utility

As part of their responses to the White House memos *Transparency and Open Government* and *Open Data Policy – Managing Information as an Asset*, all Federal agencies are examining their policies concerning data sharing and management.[37]

The establishment of standards and requirements entails the development of metadata communities with opportunities to share best practices, build consensus on metadata systems, and provide a network for scholarly communication. Federal agencies support many metadata efforts in research sciences, for example, NIH's Request for Information (RFI) for Metadata Standards and NSF's Metadata for Long-standing Large-scale Social Science Surveys program. The DOE Office of Science currently runs an initiative to guide principal investigators to incorporate data management in their evaluations. Big Data SSG agencies are examining when to mandate metadata and curation components in funded research.

Efficient and usable data interfaces are needed in the form of meta-models, metadata standards, data APIs, data type registries, persistent identifier systems, or container frameworks. These interfaces must be available for general use and tailored for domain-specific use. While data communities' needs will not be the same or use the same data model, it is likely that diverse communities will have Big Data needs and concepts that overlap. Data interfaces need to be developed that allow a wide array of communities to access data and analytical tools, but can also be flexibly modified to fit specific needs. A capability is needed in which any data stored in any location across various domain boundaries can be identified and retrieved, along with any relatable data, in response to a data request. These interfaces can provide improved capabilities to discover, search, access, consume, and deliver machine-actionable analytics insights through "mash-ups" of disparate data.

Research on effective mechanisms for data sharing should build upon existing best practices. Large-scale datasets are currently shared among communities in domains such as astronomy, genomics, physics, healthcare, and energy. Depending upon the size of the dataset and the nature of the data, many communities have already gained experience and know what processes work well and where additional or improved hardware and software resources are needed. Research to examine the resources and technologies various communities employ for data sharing will enable more effective use of resources for future development.

Work still remains to develop metadata and descriptive frameworks, as well as ontologies and taxonomies, for a wide variety of datasets from many domains. Support is needed for the development of datasets that are properly curated and include machine-readable metadata ontologies. Science funding agencies will encourage scientists and data collectors receiving Federal funding and at intramural programs to plan for the reuse of scientific data through, for example, appropriate documentation and metadata. Additionally, funding agencies will encourage coordination within the research communities of specific disciplines to collaborate and develop metadata frameworks for their respective domains. Ultimately, increased metadata curation will provide a greater return on research investments, as previously collected data will be able to serve new purposes.

Best practices for data-sharing platforms today include not only retaining and sharing data assets themselves, but also sharing the context of data collection, generation, and analysis. This process includes metadata strategies, but may also include the actual gathering techniques, analytics codes, processes, and workflows used to collect and analyze the data. In addition, the development of workflow tools that automate the capture of data provenance would be helpful. The desire to retain such useful information must be considered along with its feasibility; research is needed to help determine the balance between these two priorities. Further research is needed to determine how best to include and share contextual information when sharing datasets.

Contextual information for a dataset includes information about the processes and workflows involved in the creation of that dataset. A standardized language system, or ontology, for describing data processes is essential to enable better sharing of data. Building upon current standardization efforts, a consistent annotation system for workflows and the development of workflow registries and repositories will help communities efficiently share information about analysis processes. Related efforts have been underway over the past decade, for example, in the field of process automation for business process modeling and annotation.

Recording metadata and contextual information extends further to representing semantic information associated with data. One approach is to use top-down methods for developing controlled vocabularies, domain ontologies, and "top-level" ontologies. Another is a data-driven approach, employing natural language processing and other data-mining approaches to extract semantic information such as named entities and common relationships. Big Data SSG agencies are engaged in a number of efforts to develop domain ontologies for specific science areas. Research is needed to develop best practices for data and process annotation for different application domains, data types, and data-science scenarios.

Provide Efficient, Sustainable, and Secure Access to Data Assets

Agencies need to address the issue of data archiving by investing in research to help determine the "value" of datasets in different contexts, including supporting tools. While it is challenging to assign future value to a dataset, it is nonetheless important to develop methodologies for performing systematic cost-benefit analyses and for determining relative value among datasets. As the number of data resources increases, this task becomes more challenging. The notion of data value becomes more challenging as one searches data inventories broadly (across many resources) and deeply (finding the right data within a resource). Research is needed into intelligent, scalable, robust search methods that can keep pace with the growing library of datasets. Additionally, tools to automate the data lifecycle are needed, including tools that can aid agencies with strategic decisions about when and how datasets should be retained, archived, or deleted. The data storage, archival, and deaccessioning issues are also closely linked to advances in corresponding storage technologies. New high-density, low-cost storage solutions could make it easier in the future to store and retrieve vast amounts of data.

The United States Agency for International Development (USAID)

A BOTTOM-UP APPROACH TO FARM DATA

Small farmers can suffer because they lack the data to make crucial and timely decisions about their trade. The USAID Global Development Lab is using data systems to help farmers get the data they need.

In Senegal, a locally run farm database project has reached more than 25,000 small farmers. Data sharing and open discussion allow farmers to negotiate prices for supplies, compare farming techniques, and develop best practices. For example, farmers started measuring the spacing of plants in their fields.

By sharing this information, they identified the density that produced the highest yield and adjusted sowing practices accordingly.[38]

In Kosovo, distributing milk quality results via text message has helped over 2,035 small-scale dairy farmers by allowing buyers to set a transparent base price and offer premiums based on measurable milk quality. To date, more than 70% of the farmers have improved their milk by one or more quality grades, making the food safer and increasing revenues by 17%.

The sharing, use, and analysis of Big Data will not be limited to our immediate future. The full potential of an individual dataset may not be realized until, for example, a scientist in the distant future combines that data with another dataset that has just been collected. The Big Data ecosystem must be designed with long-term sustainability of data access in mind. How will data collected this year be available in two years, or five years? Will a tool developed today be adaptable to even larger or more complex datasets than those it was originally designed to analyze? Sustainability encompasses the development of scalable cyberinfrastructure to enable continued, uninterrupted access to data systems, even as new technologies evolve.

As emphasized in the next section, while data sharing within and across public and private sectors is a critical aspect of the Nation's collective Big Data future, issues of privacy and security are paramount in all sharing platforms. These issues must be addressed to ensure controlled and proper dissemination of data in order to engender trust among the various stakeholders and in the data. Defining data privacy and security measures will be critical elements in the advancement of Big Data sharing as well. Trust in the privacy and security measures for sensitive datasets must be integral elements of the design of any data-sharing technology, and is part of a much larger series of concerns around Big Data ethics and societal implications. Conversely, a lack of privacy and security strategies will hinder the creation or collection of data as well as reduce the potential for data sharing by degrading trust. The conclusions that can be drawn from Big Data are not limited to those gleaned by the data's original collector, but can be based on reuse and repurposing of datasets, and use of the data in combination with other datasets and for different end purposes. Thus, ensuring trust in the original datasets and derived products is essential.

The Global Earth Observation System of Systems (GEOSS)
A WORLD WITHOUT DATA BORDERS

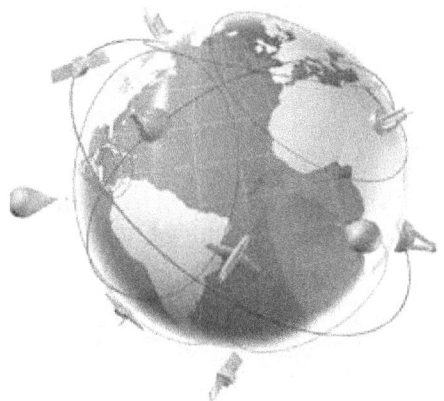

Image courtesy of the Group on Earth Observations.

Envision a world where more people will be fed, more resources will be protected, more diseases will be mitigated or even prevented, and more lives will be saved from environmental disasters.

The international Group on Earth Observations (GEO) is a voluntary partnership of 96 governments and 87 participating organizations working to develop the Global Earth Observation System of Systems (GEOSS).[39] GEOSS links international earth observation resources in the areas of agriculture, biodiversity, climate, disasters, ecosystems, energy, health, water, and weather. The goal is to provide the right Earth observation information, in the right format, to the right people, at the right time, to make the right decisions. This requires Big Data analytics, infrastructure, and principles around open data exchange. For example, early agreement on a set of data sharing and data management principles has allowed the development of open-source software to collect worldwide data on health epidemics, assess the state of global water resources, produce fire-potential maps from weather data, and calculate and communicate earthquake risk.

Thanks in part to GEO's policy advocacy and technical coordination, initiatives on data sharing have been announced in Brazil, China, Japan, South Africa, Spain, the United Kingdom, the United States, and through organizations such as the European Space Agency, the European meteorological satellite agency, and the International Council on Science.

Strategy 5: Understand Big Data collection, sharing, and use with regard to privacy, security, and ethics

Emerging Big Data technologies hold great promise for society, but also present new challenges to the ethical use of data, analyses, and results, and to the privacy and security of data. The solutions and approaches needed to address these challenges require deep attention and will have a major impact on the ability to access, share, and use Big Data.

Many large datasets originate in industry, government, and educational institutions, and are not readily accessible due to concerns about privacy or loss of competitive advantage. Privacy concerns about altering the balance of power between data collectors (often industry or government) and data providers (often individuals) challenge our ideas about public information and how such information should be equitably managed and used. Security concerns around intimate personal details of individuals have introduced new notions of harm to privacy and autonomy, and led to a demand for protections to safeguard the populace. Ethical concerns about Big Data leading to discriminatory practices and outcomes have also sparked renewed discussion on how to best enforce, for example, long-standing civil rights protections, particularly in housing, employment, and credit.[40] To address these concerns, some "rules of the road" are needed for data governance. Efforts to continue examining the implications and consequences of Big Data collection, sharing, and use are also needed.

Cybersecurity research in Big Data is supported by a variety of efforts within the Federal Government. These include the NSF's Secure and Trustworthy Cyberspace (SaTC) program [41] and the activities and investments of NITRD agencies that align with the *Federal Cybersecurity Research and Development Strategic Plan: Ensuring Prosperity and National Security.*[42] The Cybersecurity R&D Strategic Plan provides a framework for Federal R&D activities with regard to enhancing defenses against cyber threats, increasing resiliency should a threat occur, and providing ways of staying ahead of new attacks. Consequently, the intention of this section is not to provide an exhaustive list of areas for Big Data privacy and security research. Instead, it provides a set of priorities for the equitable consideration of privacy and security protections as they concern Big Data collection, sharing, and use.

Privacy research in Big Data is a national imperative. Federal agencies working under the NITRD Program are engaged in a separate, but related effort to develop a strategic plan for privacy research.[43] The effort reflects the importance of distinguishing the needs of privacy research from those of security research, and recognition that a solution in one does not necessarily protect the other. For example, poor cybersecurity is a clear threat to privacy, e.g., a hacker could breach a retailer database and gain access to private information. However, even with strong cybersecurity controls in place, privacy violations could still occur. For example, a user authorized to use a security camera system could spy on and breach the privacy rights of a co-worker.

Provide Equitable Privacy Protections

A major issue arising from Big Data is the so-called mosaic effect—as more data is made discoverable and integrated with data from other sources, there is an increased threat that seemingly disparate threads of information could be pieced together to expose private information in unanticipated ways. A growing number of studies have demonstrated the ability to identify or re-identify anonymized individuals by aggregating information from multiple publicly released datasets. To further examine this mosaic effect requires an understanding of how data can be combined that, in turn, requires systems to model the content and context of multiple datasets and how they will be used. While these are difficult technical challenges, especially when dealing with large multimedia data such as combinations that include images, videos, location data, audio, text, or graphic objects, the benefit of achieving technical solutions is that the mosaic effect could be mediated with Big Data. Limits could be specified and implemented on the combinations of data that can be accessed by certain users or classes of users. Research into automated content discovery can be important to enhance issues of privacy and confidentiality.

Many Big Data applications entail integration of data from multiple sources, each created under different policy regimes. The data may be associated with individual policies, protections, and rules of use that need to be enforced even when the data is integrated. For example, a health insurance company may partner with a social media company to combine datasets, but the two sets of data were created under very different rules of use and regulations. Handling the merger of such previously separate datasets while remaining sensitive to access and privacy needs is a critical research objective. When dealing with dynamic environments, where sources, users, applications, and data usage are continuously changing, the ability to design and evolve policies automatically and in real time will be essential to ensuring that data is readily available for use while guaranteeing data confidentiality. Research should provide technological and policy solutions for new environments and tools for managing policies dynamically; this is to ensure that the privacy of a particular dataset's contents is protected as the context surrounding it varies.

In current practice, "notice and consent" is the most widely used strategy for protecting consumer privacy. When an app is downloaded or a new online account is made, a privacy policy is displayed for the user to accept. One challenge to this paradigm is that it places the burden of privacy protection on the individual to read and understand any legal, privacy, or ethical implications. This burden is made untenable in the Big Data era where the data may be used in new, unanticipated ways. Also, data collected during transactions, or from rapidly changing sources such as social media, cannot adhere to the "notice and consent" paradigm. New conceptualizations of data privacy and protections that complement, supplement, or replace some of the traditional methods of privacy are needed. For example in February 2012, the Administration issued a report setting forth a Consumer Privacy Bill of Rights (CPBR).[44] The CPBR addresses commercial (but not public sector) uses of personal data and is a strong statement of American privacy values.[45] Research and insights into current and novel implementations of CPBR in the context of Big Data could provide a continuing framework for resolving privacy concerns.

Privacy issues with automated decisions can occur in "precision" initiatives—those that aim to provide customized individual interventions, such as precision medicine or precision education. The data that is collected in precision initiatives enable applications and decisions that can help an individual student to learn or an individual patient to recover more quickly. However, the data is sensitive because it can be falsified, stolen, or misused, which can directly impact a specific individual. There is support for new legislation in this area, for example, to protect student data privacy, while still allowing students to reap the advantages of a precision education.[46] Technological resources, such as de-identification or content- and role-based access control, have also been proposed to protect sensitive information. Research into the implications of using Big Data for precision initiatives will be important to understand the trade-offs, if any, involved in data collection. Also, research into the effectiveness of policy versus technological interventions to protect privacy will be instructive for supporting future data-driven decisions.

The quality of data-driven decisions is directly related to the quality of the original data. Therefore, some relatively new forms of data, such as data from social media, need to be evaluated for systematic sources of error. For example, recent studies have shown that people give false answers, especially in social networks, when they are unsure if their privacy is preserved. The decisions that are then made from this social media data must be evaluated in context. Research is recommended on the limitations of new data forms, on data quality, and the subsequent downstream decisions and strategies that come from that data.

DOD Defense Advanced Research Projects Agency (DARPA)
GIVING PRIVACY BY DEFAULT

Image of Louis Brandeis courtesy of the Library of Congress.

The right to privacy, coined by Louis Brandeis in 1890, was a reaction to the ability of the new "instantaneous camera" to record personal information in new ways. It seemed there was a tension between access to information and protecting privacy. Now, in the digital information age the same tension is arising due to the ease of gaining access to personal information online. The difference between Brandeis' time and today is that privacy-preserving technologies now have the potential to keep pace with the accelerating speed at which users can access data.

DARPA's Brandeis program aims to break the tension between maintaining privacy and being able to tap into the huge value of data. Specifically, Brandeis will develop tools and techniques that enable us to build systems in which private data may be used only for its intended purpose and no other. The potential for impact is dramatic. Assured data privacy can open the doors to personal medicine, effective smart cities, detailed global data, and fine-grained Internet awareness. Without strong privacy controls, every one of these possibilities would face systematic opposition.

Privacy-enhancing technologies that enable computation on data in such a way that an individual's contribution cannot be revealed might be one approach to eliminating the need for users to consent to data use. A range of technologies aims to preserve privacy based on cryptographic techniques such as identity-based encryption, attribute-based encryption, homomorphic encryption, "zero-knowledge" systems, secure multiparty computation, oblivious RAM, multi-input functional encryption, and others. Research support must continue in these areas and will need to address issues of scalability, as well as lack of adoption of these technologies within enterprise-scale applications.

Enable a Secure Big Data Cyberspace

In the cyberspace context of Big Data, data may flow among many different data systems and sub-systems. The overall security of the entire network of systems is critical as well as the security of the individual system components. *Trustworthy Cyberspace: Strategic Plan for the Federal Cybersecurity Research and Development Program* discussed the idea of tailored trustworthy systems, where the system recognizes the user's context and evolves as the context evolves.[47] However, organizations would have to design methods that monitor the data security of a network of changing trustworthy systems to ensure that the combined system is still secure. For example, if a trusted credit card system is linked to a trusted report-generation tool, then there should be a reliable way to ensure that the combined system is still equally secure from cyber-attacks. Research is needed to provide the tools for monitoring cybersecurity as data passes through a large number of potentially changing sub-systems.

There is a reciprocal opportunity for Big Data technologies to contribute to research in cybersecurity. Research is needed to enable the use of security-related data (e.g., network traffic, detailed device internal state information) to enhance the security of information and networking technologies.

Understand Ethics for Sound Data Governance

In the past, agencies have benefitted by supporting research into the Ethical, Legal, and Social Implications (ELSI) of transformative areas, such as genetic engineering or nanotechnology. The NIH has a 20-year research program in the Ethical, Legal, and Social Implications of genomics within the National Human Genome Research Institute[48] and the cross-agency National Nanotechnology Initiative has sponsored two nanotechnology Centers of Excellence that focus specifically on ELSI issues, with support from DOE, NASA, NIH, NIST, USGS, and other agencies.[49] The benefits of these and other programs have been to connect science to the rest of society by identifying best practices and uncovering value-sensitive consequences associated with specific research. These same benefits should be reflected in Big Data research through the creation of an ELSI research agenda for Big Data.

Data-driven decisions are becoming more common in the workplace as data is used for activities such as performance tracking, workplace evaluation, operations, benefits eligibility determination, employment, and prescribing. Disputes over employer-collected data have become part of the bargaining process between worker unions and some major corporations, specifically on questions of whether disciplinary actions should be taken based solely on data, or if data can be collected without employee knowledge.

Large-scale use of automated decision-making tools, such as scores and algorithms in Big Data systems, must be investigated specifically to understand the impact that such tools have on the private as well as public sectors.[50] As human experts are partially or completely replaced by automated decision-making algorithms, it will be important to support research on the quality of data-driven decisions in the workplace. This research will address how these automated decision systems affect issues such as the flexibility and reliability of organizational processes, the nature of workers' subject matter knowledge and expertise, organizational memory and learning, job characteristics, employment opportunities, workforce re-training, and human auditing or appeal. In addition, research is needed into how these factors are balanced with elements like reduced costs or increased quality of products or services.

Big Data ethics research will help determine the guidelines and policies for working with Big Data. Data governance requires balancing different types of risk relationships, i.e., Big Data might increase privacy risks in some domains but reduce security risks in others (e.g., national security). Ethical models for these different types of risks are necessary to identify suitable trade-offs. In particular, all Big Data users must pay careful attention that Big Data does not consistently propagate errors or systematically disadvantage certain groups, whether inadvertently or intentionally. Individuals and groups can also be unknowingly put at risk from voluntary data collection. For example, family history data for one member of a family can be sufficient to infer disease susceptibility of other members of the same family or even ethnic group. Currently, the 2008 Genetic Information Nondiscrimination Act (GINA) provides Federal protection from genetic discrimination in health insurance and employment. Other forms of Big Data may need similar protections around appropriate use and warrant detailed investigation to inform the public as well as policymakers.

NSF Directorate for Computer and Information Science and Engineering (CISE)

BUILDING AN ETHICAL ROADMAP

Big Data is big not only because of the size of the data but also the number of people involved and affected by the data. New opportunities for education and healthcare, as well as disruptive business paradigms, can raise major ethical concerns for schools and students, hospitals and patients, businesses and workers, and the government and citizens.

The Council for Big Data, Ethics, and Society[51] was developed, with funding from NSF CISE, to provide critical social and cultural perspectives on Big Data initiatives. The Council brings together researchers from diverse disciplines to examine the issues and help develop mutually agreed-upon frameworks to help researchers, practitioners, and the public understand the social, ethical, legal, and policy issues surrounding the Big Data phenomenon. To date, the Council has released reports on data ethics, data management, and the history and development of ethics codes in related fields.

The Council provides the structure necessary to coordinate scholars and develop social and ethical research initiatives in Big Data. The Council's work will lead to new research projects and help shape future research agendas in Big Data to benefit society and science.

Who is the "owner" of a piece of data is often a difficult legal question to answer. Multiple stakeholders could be associated with any data item, each with different (possibly conflicting) objectives. Furthermore, not all stakeholders may be known to each other. For example, a dataset user (and thus a stakeholder for that data) may not be aware that a law-enforcement agency is also using the same data. Solutions need to be investigated to eliminate conflicts and balance data utility with data ethics. Efforts to explore ethics-sensitive research, i.e. research that is explicitly attentive to the values, needs, and goals of multiple stakeholder groups, would enable stakeholders to dynamically consider common elements like data utility, risk, and cost, alongside values and societal ethics. This interplay of utility and ethics connects science to the larger society in ways that represent and empower our national ideals.

In general, solutions that address the complex issues of Big Data privacy, security, and ethics may not result in a "one size fits all" model. Because different domains may possess different definitions of data utility, multiple dimensions may need to be tailored for different application domains to achieve practical solutions. Therefore, identifying and responding to the needs of specific communities will be critical in resolving the toughest Big Data privacy, security, and ethical concerns.

> *Strategy 6: Improve the national landscape for Big Data education and training to fulfill increasing demand for both deep analytical talent and analytical capacity for the broader workforce*

Big Data and the field of data science are flourishing. Many surveys and studies have identified a shortage in the number of people with relevant Big Data skill sets and the need for more training and formal education programs in data science. To meet the demand, educational institutions are working to establish programs at all levels.

The need is for both domain experts who are trained in data science and "core" data scientists who focus on data science as their primary field of expertise. Individuals educated in data science at the undergraduate and graduate levels are vital to meeting needs across all sectors—industry, government, and academia. The core specialists in Big Data include data science researchers, information scientists, statisticians, computer scientists, database and software programmers, curators, librarians, and archivists with specialization in data science. The National Science Board emphasized the importance of these experts to the successful management and analyses of digital data collections.[52] Research investments are needed to expand the current pipeline of support to the field of data science and provide direction on the necessary competencies for the development and training of future core data scientists. The National Science Foundation Research Traineeship program, for example, has a priority interdisciplinary research theme on Data-Enabled Science and Engineering (DESE).

The challenge of producing a properly trained workforce with Big Data skills is enormous. Integrating data science—the field of study focused on data foundations, tools, and techniques—throughout our Nation's education system is essential to developing a workforce that can address our national priorities across domains and sectors. Additionally, as more industries take advantage of Big Data to accelerate discovery and develop new products and services, it is in our national interest to meet the increased workforce demand to ensure that the United States remains economically competitive.

To build the human capacity for Big Data research, development, and implementation and expand the current data science landscape requires a multi-faceted approach. Education and training strategies could include the core technical facets of data science that originate from multiple traditional domains, such as statistics, machine learning, data mining, visualization, and ethics. Such strategies could target the training of new data scientists, and also increase the data science competencies and skillsets of current professionals.

Continue Growing the Cadre of Data Scientists

There has been a groundswell of new Data Science programs offered at institutions that teach the necessary skills for dealing with Big Data. Many of these programs are at the Master's level, but the number of programs at the undergraduate and Ph.D. levels is increasing. A core data science curriculum includes course material from computer science, statistics, ethics, social science, and policy. In addition to Data Science programs at undergraduate and graduate levels, programs are emerging to train students from other disciplines in the basics of data science. These disciplines cover the full range from science, engineering, biomedicine, clinical medicine, business, social science, humanities, law, and the arts. Consensus about the program content is beginning to emerge. Big Data SSG agencies can play a significant role in helping define the needs and requirements for these programs. In conjunction with the National Research Council's Committee on Applied and Theoretical Statistics (CATS), NSF brought together the community at a workshop entitled "Training Students to Extract Value from Big Data" to discuss how to educate and train students in order to increase the cadre of data scientists.

Growing and sustaining R&D investments in Big Data helps advance the field of data science and support the training for the next generation of core data scientists. Funding in the form of competitive grants to academic institutions will help train faculty, post-doctoral scholars, graduate students, and undergraduates in cutting edge data science technology. In particular, funding that allows more graduate students to engage in data science research at academic institutions will enable both the research needed to advance the field and the training needed to grow a cohort of core data scientists.

As the field of Big Data continues to grow and evolve, coordination will be necessary to assess educational needs. The education and training community will help determine how to structure the data science curricula and how to reallocate educational resources to meet the demand for specific skillsets. At this early stage, maintaining agility and flexibility in undergraduate as well as graduate curricula and programs is necessary to ensure that cutting-edge concepts and techniques are being incorporated.

As data-science programs grow, it is essential that the pedagogy encourage the participation of women, underrepresented minorities, and persons with disabilities. These populations are significantly underrepresented in computer science; therefore, data science education should proactively develop and evolve to incorporate broad participation. For example, curricula that emphasize the role of Big Data for "social good" in both formal and informal education settings have demonstrated success at engaging greater proportions of women and underrepresented minorities.[53] Also, curricula that actively foster collaboration have proved successful at increasing productivity, retention, and success of women and underrepresented minority scientists in multiple Science, Technology, Engineering, and Mathematics (STEM) fields.

As data-science curricula expand and diversify content, universities and colleges should be prepared to accommodate additional students by increasing the number of advanced degree programs in data science. To date, there are approximately 60 institutions that offer a Master's degree program in data science, but more programs and teachers are needed.[54] Agencies can also institute awards that honor data scientists who exemplify the role of teacher-scholars through outstanding research, excellent education, and the integration of education and research.

Expand the Community of Data-Empowered Domain Experts

Domain researchers, in fields outside of computer science and statistics, would benefit from financial support to supplement their expertise with discipline-specific data science training. Such researchers come from many different data-enabled fields, from science and engineering, to social science, humanities, and law. Educating these researchers to utilize Big Data provides them the opportunity to enhance the work within their own disciplines. A 2014 National Academies of Science report explains that there exists an expertise gap between domain and data scientists. Domain scientists lack knowledge about the technologies that are available and relevant to their work while data scientists have not considered additional domains where their work is relevant.[55]

To bridge this gap between domain and data scientists and support the utilization of increasingly data-rich research, support can be expanded for projects that require interdisciplinary teams to devise solutions. These collaborations will enable domain scientists to access resources and learn the tools to incorporate large datasets within their research. Additionally, agencies could encourage universities to incorporate Big Data challenges posed by industry experts into a practicum to complement the data science curriculum. One model of this approach is the NSF-sponsored eScience Institute at the University of Washington. The eScience Institute currently supports collaborative challenges posed by industry experts by offering training, curricula, fellowships, and seminars to answer real-world data problems. Fostering an environment for multi-sector partnerships to grow and thrive will accelerate innovation and expand the impact of Federal investments.

NIH Big Data to Knowledge (BD2K) Initiative
EXPANDING DATA SCIENCE CAPABILITY ACROSS BIOMEDICINE

A current bottleneck in the development of health knowledge is the ability of the workforce to efficiently manage and fully analyze large amounts of complex data. A data-savvy workforce is necessary for advancing biomedical science, improving health knowledge, and developing successful strategies to combat disease.

Big Data to Knowledge (BD2K)[56] is a trans-NIH initiative established to enable biomedical research as a digital research enterprise, to facilitate discovery and support new knowledge, and to foster data science skills in the biomedical workforce. Biomedical data science pre-doctoral students, postdocs, and researchers are being trained to develop and use new tools and methods.

An essential element of the Initiative is the multi-institutional BD2K Centers consortium. Each Center addresses distinct biomedical research challenges, but they all include workforce training and collaboration components. Together with the other BD2K training activities, these training strategies are essential to accelerate advancements in health and well-being in an era where biomedical research is increasingly analytical and more data rich than any time in prior history.

Domain science educators often have limited flexibility to enhance their academic curriculum with the full data science core curriculum. In these cases, domain science students can benefit from a general data science foundation delivered through data science short-term courses, or modules. These courses can be developed to incorporate real-world application of theory to improve course engagement and relevancy. For example, scientists and students in specialized data science courses could work as a class to develop algorithms to address research questions in a particular domain, for example energy grid demands, water usage in agriculture, or human microbiome populations.

Domain scientists would also benefit from initiatives to supplement their training with data science through seed grants, professional development stipends, internships, fellowships, and summer research experiences. NSF recently announced an NSF Research Traineeship (NRT) program designed to encourage the development and implementation of transformative and scalable models for STEM graduate education training. The NRT program includes a Traineeship Track dedicated to effective training of STEM graduate students in high-priority interdisciplinary research areas, through the use of a comprehensive traineeship model that is innovative, evidence-based, scalable, and aligned with changing workforce and research needs. Additionally, NSF is catalyzing the growth of data science infrastructure and data scientists by leveraging existing programs to incorporate data science training into their solicitations.[57]

The NIH is implementing strategies to train domain researchers to engage with Big Data. In May 2015, NIH announced the first round of Big Data to Knowledge (BD2K) Institutional Training Grant awards, which provide undergraduate and graduate students with integrated training in computer science, informatics, statistics, mathematics, and biomedical science. The NIH BD2K program will also offer awards to support an effective and diverse biomedical data science workforce by supporting educational resource development, training opportunities, and public engagement projects.

Broaden the Data-Capable Workforce

Many of the skills that are essential for working with Big Data include basic competency in data preparation, simple data visualization, basic descriptive statistics, and data characterization. Indeed, these essential skills, which sometimes occupy 70-80% of the time involved in analyzing Big Data, are often overlooked in data analysis. There is a demand for workforce trained to collect, record, extract, clean, and annotate data.[58] Community colleges, two-year colleges, certificate programs, and intensive workshops can provide opportunities for students and professionals to acquire the necessary data preparation and analysis skills for a small investment of their time and money. Such basic education and training initiatives are especially pertinent to workforce professionals and managers interested in expanding their professional skills. This level of data science training could also be a component of programs for Veterans returning to the workforce and as re-entry opportunities for the unemployed. Community colleges and 2-year academic institutions could address the need for knowledge workers in Big Data by developing data science tracks to prepare their graduates for either job readiness or advancement to a bachelor's degree in data science. These institutions could also support cross training, recycling skills, and re-entry programs to expand the workforce base in Big Data.

National Aeronautics and Space Administration (NASA)

WE ARE ALL DATA SCIENTISTS

Image courtesy of the National Aeronautics and Space Administration.

Is there life beyond this planet? Can students experience what it is like to be an astronaut on the Moon? What is the air quality and water temperature like around the world? Today's technologies allow citizens to explore and contribute to these types of questions once reserved for scientists.

NASA has a long-standing involvement with citizen science. Pioneering projects like SETI@Home and GalaxyZoo gave millions of participants the ability to help search for extraterrestrial life and classify heavenly objects. Current NASA hack-a-thons and challenges invite citizens to explore audio files to help re-live past space missions or create space games to mimic working on different planets. In 2014, a group of citizen scientists successfully established communication with an inactive 35-year-old NASA spacecraft in an attempt to renew its scientific mission.

NASA and the National Science Foundation (NSF), with support from NOAA and the Department of State, jointly fund the Global Learning and Observations to Benefit the Environment (GLOBE) Program that connects schools, students, and teachers worldwide in measuring data about the Earth, such as air quality, water temperature, and freshwater animals. Using a GLOBE visualization tool, they can map, graph, filter, and export data that has been measured across GLOBE protocols since 1995. Another initiative, known as My NASA DATA, provides schools with satellite data and lesson plans to engage students in atmospheric science and introduce them to data analysis.

Improve the Public's Data Literacy

A data-driven world requires a citizenry that is data literate. This includes the ability to read, correctly interpret, and communicate information from data, as well as create data and knowledge derived from other data. Data science education at the K-12 levels can assist in providing nationwide data literacy, while also preparing students for more advanced data science concepts and course work after high school. There are numerous opportunities for the data science research community to engage with K-12 education, and Big Data SSG agencies should encourage more of them. Access should be provided to data science educational resources, such as textbooks, online courses, practicums, challenges, and citizen science projects, in order to help increase data literacy. A college education should not be a prerequisite to acquiring data literacy.

To date, very few public high schools offer data science coursework. Continued research in data science education is necessary to explore the basics of data literacy and should incorporate rigorous assessments and evaluations. What curricular models help build effective data literacy? Which data science skills should be taught at the various grade levels? Additionally, as the K-12 education system begins to expand its data science curriculum, professional development opportunities for teachers will be needed that are short in duration, offer data science kits, and enable easy integration into existing curricula. The data science curricula should also make use of open-source data science tools in order to accommodate the varied technological infrastructure in public schools.

For example, one high school data science course is currently being piloted in the Los Angeles Unified School District. In 2014, the district offered their first Introducing Data Science (IDS) course in ten high schools to address the data science talent shortage. The IDS course was designed to provide a meaningful and alternative pathway for math requirements while providing a strategy to prepare students for new job skills. The course is easily incorporated into the Common Core standards and has approval from the University of California system to count as a math course and statistics course for pre-admission requirements.

Strategy 7: *Create and enhance connections in the national Big Data innovation ecosystem*

To enable sustained engagements at the Federal level, involving tangible, measurable goals, the NITRD Big Data SSG is seeking ways to lower communications barriers and create agile collaboration mechanisms. There is strong interest both in removing bureaucratic hurdles to enable technology and data sharing and in building lasting programs with sustainable funding models, involving interagency collaborations as well as collaborations with industry.

Encourage Cross-Sector, Cross-Agency Big Data Collaborations

Big Data SSG agencies support collaborative activities across all sectors—government, industry, not-for-profits, academia, and the general public. In 2013, the Big Data SSG organized a White House-sponsored "Data to Knowledge to Action" event, which launched over 30 new multi-sector collaborations involving some 90 partners across the public and private sectors. Additional collaborative activities that have grown out of the Big Data R&D Initiative include: the release of an NSF and NIH joint solicitation, "Core Techniques and Technologies for Big Data;" NASA, NSF, and DOE working with Topcoder to run a series of ideation challenges around data fusion; NASA working with Amazon.com to provide access to earth science data with the NASA Earth Exchange; NOAA working with a consortium consisting of Amazon, IBM, and the Open Cloud Consortium to release all NOAA data for public access; and the NSF Innovation Transition (InTrans) awards that facilitate transition of research results to practice, with industry sponsorship.

In 2015, NSF launched the Big Data Regional Innovation Hubs program (BD Hubs) to foster regional, cross-sector collaborations and multi-sector projects to foster innovation with Big Data. As a complement to the institutional gateways, the regional hubs provide the ability to engage with local or regional stakeholders, e.g., city, county, and state governments, as well as permit a focus on regional issues. These collaborative activities and partnerships play a critical role in building and sustaining a successful national Big Data innovation ecosystem.

The Big Data SSG also identified the need for "development testbeds" or "sandboxes" to enable conversion of agency-funded R&D results into innovative production capabilities, as well as for engaging in proofs of concept with both open source and proprietary commercial off-the-shelf solutions. Such a program would enable the sharing of experiences, results, and capabilities among agencies, shorten the development phase of a project, and allow agencies to assimilate and integrate new results and solutions quickly. Industry engagement in the program would demonstrate broader utility, foster better interoperability, and potentially provide long-term sustainability of solutions. Pilots and testbed infrastructure could be shared among agencies, thereby helping to maximize investments and share the benefits of projects and technologies that would otherwise remain isolated within a particular agency.

Promote Policies and Frameworks for Faster Responses and Measurable Impacts

Agile mechanisms should be developed to enable rapid and dynamic coalescing of stakeholders—across agencies and with industry—in response to urgent priorities. For example, after the Deep Water Horizon oil spill event, NOAA, USGS, EPA, DHS, DOE, and others collaborated to bring together timely information from diverse sources, from satellite imagery to sampling sites, in order to inform a rapid response to the crisis. In the future, policies must be put in place so that agencies with relevant data and resources for addressing the problem can be quickly assembled, together with industry, academia, and non-profit partners, where needed, to leverage a data inventory and common knowledge base that cuts across agency operations, along with open source as well as proprietary tools for analysis. Processes should be put in place so that useful products generated by such rapid response teams are adopted and sustained when operations return to normal.

Materials Genome Initiative (MGI)
MATERIALS FOR THE FUTURE

Materials make a difference. Human health and welfare, clean energy, and national security are all pressing needs of our time, but all have underlying challenges whose solutions require advanced materials. For example, packaging that keeps food fresher and more nutritious, new lightweight materials for vehicles that significantly improve fuel efficiency, or solar cells as cheap as paint would be game changing. Yet, it can take 20 years or more and millions of dollars to move a new material from discovery to the market.

The Materials Genome Initiative (MGI) is a multi-agency initiative designed to create a new era of advanced materials. The aim is to use Big Data techniques and multiple agencies' research capacity to discover, develop, manufacture, and deploy advanced materials twice as fast as possible today and at a fraction of the cost. Since the launch of MGI in 2011, the Federal government has invested over $250 million in new R&D and innovation infrastructure to anchor the use of advanced materials in existing and emerging industrial sectors in the United States. Nine Federal agencies are cooperatively sponsoring workshops and joint meetings of principal investigators to enhance research coordination.

Currently, Big Data is enabling advanced applications that are, in many cases, outpacing the policy regimes under which they operate. Agencies foresee the need for a venue that includes industry for discussing policies governing Big Data use. The policies must keep pace with technological innovation and the new applications made possible by the technology.

Support is needed for metrics and benchmarks to assess trends in technology and outcomes of policies. Both system- and application-level benchmarks and analysis can be used to help determine where improvements are called for, improve performance, establish interoperability requirements, and determine the types of computing systems required. For example, they can help analyze response times under real-world conditions and help create a community of practice around a range of Big Data performance metrics. For example, in the past, metrics and benchmarks were successfully created to study network interoperability.

And, finally, to increase the impact of Big Data research investments, the research enterprise should be linked with end users early in the project lifecycle. Such connections can help speed the transition of technology from the lab to operations, while maintaining a strong foundation of exploratory, curiosity-driven research. Practitioner communities need support as they progress through a series of engagements with Big Data researchers and participate in Big Data challenge competitions. Each step requires tangible, measurable targets in order to create a process for achieving significant results on grand challenge problems through the use of Big Data.

Acronyms

AI – Artificial Intelligence
API – Application Programming Interface
ASCR – DOE's Advanced Scientific Computing Research Program
BD2K – NIH's Big Data to Knowledge Initiative
BRAP – NSF's Benchmarks of Realistic Scientific Application Performance of Large-Scale Computing Systems Program
DARPA – Defense Advanced Research Projects Agency
DHS – Department of Homeland Security
DOE – Department of Energy
ESnet – DOE's Energy Sciences Network
GEM – Global Earthquake Model
GENI – NSF's Global Environment for Networking Innovations Project
GEO – International Group on Earth Observations or NSF's Geosciences Directorate
GEOSS – Global Earth Observation System of Systems
GINA – Genetic Information Nondiscrimination Act
GLOBE – Global Learning and Observations to Benefit the Environment Program
IoT – Internet of Things
ITL – NIST's Information and Technology Laboratory
MGI – Materials Genome Initiative
NASA – National Aeronautics and Space Administration
NIH – National Institutes of Health
NIST – National Institute of Standards and Technology
NITRD – Networking and Information Technology Research and Development Program
NOAA – National Oceanic and Atmospheric Administration
NRT – NSF's Research Traineeship Program
NSF – National Science Foundation
NSTC – National Science and Technology Council
OFR – Office of Financial Research
OMB – Office of Management and Budget
PCAST – President's Council of Advisors on Science and Technology
RFI – Request for Information
SaTC – NSF's Secure and Trustworthy Cyberspace Program
STEM – Science, Technology, Engineering, and Mathematics
USAID – U.S. Agency for International Development
USGEO – U.S. Group on Earth Observations
USGS – U.S. Geological Survey

References

[1] The following definition is consistent with the usage of the term throughout this document: *Big Data is a term for datasets that are so large or complex that traditional data processing applications are inadequate. Challenges include analysis, capture, data curation, search, sharing, storage, transfer, visualization, querying, and information privacy. The term often refers simply to the use of predictive analytics or certain other advanced methods to extract value from data, and seldom to a particular size of dataset. Accuracy in big data may lead to more confident decision making, and better decisions can result in greater operational efficiency, cost reduction, and reduced risk.* Wikipedia, 22 Apr. 2016.

[2] "Obama Administration Unveils 'Big Data' Initiative: Announces $200 Million in New R&D Investments." *The White House*. Web. 23 Oct. 2015. <https://www.whitehouse.gov/sites/default/files/microsites/ostp/big_data_press_release_final_2.pdf>.

[3] "The National Big Data R&D Initiative," *NITRD Big Data Senior Steering Group*. Web. 26 Oct. 2015. <https://www.nitrd.gov/bigdata/documents/NationalBigDataRDInitiativeVisionAndActions.pdf>.

[4] Obama Administration Unveils 'Big Data' Initiative: Announces $200 Million in New R&D Investments." *The White House*. Web. 23 Oct. 2015. <https://www.whitehouse.gov/sites/default/files/microsites/ostp/big_data_press_release_final_2.pdf>.

[5] "Data to Knowledge to Action: Building new Partnerships," *National Coordinating Office/NITRD* Web 12 Nov. 2013. https://www.nitrd.gov/nitrdgroups/index.php?title=Data_to_Knowledge_to_Action

[6] "Report to the President and Congress Ensuring Leadership in Federally Funded Research and Development in Information Technology." *President's Council of Advisors on Science and Technology*. Web. 30 Sept. 2015. <https://www.whitehouse.gov/sites/default/files/microsites/ostp/PCAST/nitrd_report_aug_2015.pdf>.

[7] Hart, David. "On the Origins of Google," *National Science Foundation*. Web. 21 Oct. 2015. <https://www.nsf.gov/discoveries/disc_summ.jsp?cntn_id=100660>.

[8] "SciDAC's FastBit Bitmap Indexing Technology Receives R&D 100 Award," *Department of Energy/Office of Science*. Web. 21 Oct. 2015. <http://science.energy.gov/ascr/research/fast-bit/>.

[9] Preuss, Paul. "Understanding What's Up With the Higgs Boson," *Lawrence Berkeley Lab*. Web. 21 Oct. 2015. <http://newscenter.lbl.gov/2012/06/28/higgs-2012/>.

[10] "Executive Order—Creating a National Strategic Computing Initiative." *The White House*. Web. 30 Sept. 2015. <https://www.whitehouse.gov/the-press-office/2015/07/29/executive-order-creating-national-strategic-computing-initiative>.

[11] "Accelerating Scientific Knowledge Discovery." *Department of Energy/Office of Science*. Web. 30 Sept. 2015. <http://science.energy.gov/~/media/ascr/pdf/program-documents/docs/ASKD_Report_V1_0.pdf>; "Synergistic Challenges in Data-Intensive Science and Exascale Computing." *Department of Energy/Office of Science*. Web. 30 Sept. 2015. <http://science.energy.gov/~/media/ascr/ascac/pdf/reports/2013/ASCAC_Data_Intensive_Computing_report_final.pdf>.

[12] "What is GENI?" *Geni: Exploring Networks of the Future*. Web. 30 Sept. 2015. <https://www.geni.net/?page_id=2>.

[13] "What is US Ignite?" *US Ignite*. Web. 30 Sept. 2015. <https://www.us-ignite.org/about/what-is-us-ignite>.

[14] "The Zettabyte Era: Trends and Analysis," *Cisco*. Web. 30 Sept. 2015. <http://www.cisco.com/c/en/us/solutions/collateral/service-provider/visual-networking-index-vni/VNI_Hyperconnectivity_WP.pdf>.

[15] "About NEON," *NEON*. Web. 30 Sept. 2015. <http://www.neoninc.org/about/>.

[16] "Discovery with Data: Leveraging Statistics with Computer Science to Transform Science and Society," *American Statistical Association*. Web. 30 Sept. 2015. <http://www.amstat.org/policy/pdfs/BigDataStatisticsJune2014.pdf>.

[17] "The White House BRAIN Initiative." *The White House*. Web. 21 Oct. 2015. <https://www.whitehouse.gov/BRAIN>.

[18] "The Story So Far," *Galaxy Zoo*. 30 Sept. 2015. <http://www.galaxyzoo.org/#/story>.

[19] "The Science Behind Foldit," *Foldit: Solve Puzzles for Science*. Web. 30 Sept. 2015. <https://fold.it/portal/info/about>.

[20] "Designing a Digital Future: Federally Funded Research and Development in Networking and Information Technology." *President's Council of Advisors on Science and Technology.* Web. 30 Sept. 2015. <http://www.whitehouse.gov/sites/default/files/microsites/ostp/pcast-nitrd2013.pdf>.

[21] "Guidelines for Ensuring and Maximizing the Quality, Objectivity, Utility, and Integrity of Information Disseminated by Federal Agencies." *Office of Management and Budget, The White House.* Web. 30 Sept. 2015. <https://www.whitehouse.gov/omb/fedreg_final_information_quality_guidelines/>.

[22] Guba, Egon G. "Criteria for Assessing the Trustworthiness of Naturalistic Inquiries." Educational Communication and Technology, USA: Springer 1981. Vol. 29, No. 2, pp. 75-91. <http://www.jstor.org/stable/30219811>.

[23] "Principles and Guidelines for Reporting Preclinical Research." *National Institutes of Health.* Web. 30 Sept. 2015. <http://www.nih.gov/about/reporting-preclinical-research.htm>.

[24] MD Shaw LJ, Miller DD, Romeis JC, Kargl D, Younis LT, Chaitman BR. *Gender Differences in the Noninvasive Evaluation and Management of Patients with Suspected Coronary Artery Disease.* Annals of Internal Medicine, 1994, Vol 120, No. 7.

[25] "Synergistic Challenges in Data-Intensive Science and Exascale Computing: DOE ASCAC Data Subcommittee Report, March 2013." *Department of Energy Office of Science.* Web. 30 Sept. 2015. <http://science.energy.gov/~/media/ascr/ascac/pdf/reports/2013/ASCAC_Data_Intensive_Computing_report_final.pdf>.

[26] "Data Crosscutting Requirements Review: DOE ASCR Report April 2013." *Department of Energy Office of Science.* Web. 30 Sept. 2015. <http://science.energy.gov/~/media/ascr/pdf/program-documents/docs/ASCR_DataCrosscutting2_8_28_13.pdf>.

[27] "BER Virtual Laboratory: Innovative Framework for Biological and Environmental Grand Challenges: A Report from the Biological and Environmental Research Advisory Committee February 2013." *Department of Energy Office of Science.* Web. 30 Sept. 2015. <http://science.energy.gov/~/media/ber/berac/pdf/Reports/BER_VirtualLaboratory_finalwebHR.pdf>.

[28] "Executive Order—Creating a National Strategic Computing Initiative." *The White House.* Web. 30 Sept. 2015. <https://www.whitehouse.gov/the-press-office/2015/07/29/executive-order-creating-national-strategic-computing-initiative>.

[29] "Big Data Study Group." *National Institute of Standards and Technology (NIST).* Web. 30 Sept. 2015. <http://jtc1bigdatasg.nist.gov/home.php>.

[30] Bristol, R. Sky; Euliss, Ned H. Jr.; Booth, Nathaniel L.; Burkardt, Nina; Diffendorfer, Jay E.; Gesch, Dean B.; McCallum, Brian E.; Miller, David M.; Morman, Suzette A.; Poore, Barbara S.; Signell, Richard P.; and Viger, Roland J. "U.S. Geological Survey Core Science Systems Strategy—Characterizing, Synthesizing, and Understanding the Critical Zone through a Modular Science Framework." *U.S. Geological Survey.* Web. 30 Sept. 2015. <http://pubs.usgs.gov/circ/1383b/>.

[31] See Strategy 4 for more information on sharing and Strategy 7 for more specifics on cooperation.

[32] "Benchmarks of Realistic Scientific Application Performance of Large-Scale Computing System (BRAP)." *National Science Foundation Division of Advanced Cyberinfrastructure.* Web. 30 Sept. 2015. <http://www.nsf.gov/funding/pgm_summ.jsp?pims_id=505151>.

[33] "Big Data Top 100 Project," *Big Date Top 100: An open, community-based effort for benchmarking big data systems.* Web. 30 Sept. 2015. <http://www.bigdatatop100.org/about>.

[34] "Building Community and Capacity in Data Intensive Research in Education (BCC-EHR)." *National Science Foundation Directorate for Social, Behavioral & Economic Sciences (SBE).* Web. 30 Sept. 2015. <http://www.nsf.gov/publications/pub_summ.jsp?ods_key=nsf15563&org=SBE>.

[35] "The Commons: An Overview." *Data Science at the National Institutes of Health (NIH).* Web. 30 Sept. 2015. <https://datascience.nih.gov/commons>.

[36] *Frontiers in Massive Data Analysis*, National Research Council, The National Academies Press, 2013 page 41.

[37] "Transparency and Open Government." *The White House.* Web. 30 Sept. 2015. <https://www.whitehouse.gov/the_press_office/TransparencyandOpenGovernment> and "Open Data Policy—Managing Information as an Asset." *Office of Management and Budget, Federal Chief Information Officer, U.S. Chief Technology Officer, Office of Information and Regulatory Affairs.* Web. 30 Sept. 2015. <https://www.whitehouse.gov/sites/default/files/omb/memoranda/2013/m-13-13.pdf>.

[38] "Turning Data into Action." USAID U.S. Global Development Lab. Web. 30 Sept. 2015. <http://www.usaid.gov/sites/default/files/documents/15396/Data2Action.pdf>.

[39] "About GEOSS: The Global Earth Observation System of Systems." *Group on Earth Observations*. Web. 30 Sept. 2015. <http://www.earthobservations.org/geoss.php>.

[40] "Fact Sheet: Big Data and Privacy Working Group Review." *The White House.* Web. 30 Sept. 2015. <https://www.whitehouse.gov/the-press-office/2014/05/01/fact-sheet-big-data-and-privacy-working-group-review>.

[41] "Secure and Trustworthy Cyberspace (SaTC)." *National Science Foundation*. Web. 30 Sept. 2015. <http://www.nsf.gov/publications/pub_summ.jsp?ods_key=nsf15575&org=NSF>.

[42] "Federal Cybersecurity Research and Development Strategic Plan: Ensuring Prosperity and National Security." *National Science and Technology Council.* Web. 25 April. 2016. <https://www.whitehouse.gov/sites/whitehouse.gov/files/documents/2016_Federal_Cybersecurity_Research_and_Development_Stratgeic_Plan.pdf>.

[43] "National Privacy Research Strategy." *The Networking and Information Technology Research and Development (NITRD) Program.* Web. 30 Sept. 2015. <https://www.nitrd.gov/cybersecurity/nationalprivacyresearchstrategy.aspx>.

[44] "Administration Discussion Draft: Consumer Privacy Bill of Rights Act." *The White House*. Web. 30 Sept. 2015. <https://www.whitehouse.gov/sites/default/files/omb/legislative/letters/cpbr-act-of-2015-discussion-draft.pdf>.

[45] "Report to the President: Big Data and Privacy: A Technological Perspective." *President's Council of Advisors on Science and Technology*. Web. 30 Sept. 2015. <https://www.whitehouse.gov/sites/default/files/microsites/ostp/PCAST/pcast_big_data_and_privacy_-_may_2014.pdf>.

[46] "Promoting Innovation and Protecting Privacy in the Classroom." *The White House*. Web. 30 Sept. 2015. <https://www.whitehouse.gov/blog/2014/10/09/promoting-innovation-and-protecting-privacy-classroom>.

[47] "Trustworthy Cyberspace: Strategic Plan for the Federal Cybersecurity Research and Development Program." *National Science and Technology Council.* Web. 30 Sept. 2015. <https://www.whitehouse.gov/sites/default/files/microsites/ostp/fed_cybersecurity_rd_strategic_plan_2011.pdf>.

[48] "The Ethical, Legal and Social Implications (ELSI) Research Program." *National Institutes of Health National Human Genome Research Institute.* Web. 30 Sept. 2015. <http://www.genome.gov/elsi/>.

[49] "Ethical, Legal, and Societal Issues." *National Nanotechnology Initiative*. Web. 30 Sept. 2015. <http://www.nano.gov/you/ethical-legal-issues>.

[50] "Big Data: Seizing Opportunities, Preserving Values." *The White House*. Web. 30 Sept. 2015. <https://www.whitehouse.gov/sites/default/files/docs/big_data_privacy_report_5.1.14_final_print.pdf>.

[51] "Council for Big Data, Ethics, and Society." *Council for Big Data, Ethics, and Society.* Web. 30 Sept. 2015. <http://bdes.datasociety.net/>.

[52] "National Science Board: Long-Lived Digital Data Collections: Enabling Research and Education in the 21st Century." 2005, *National Science Foundation*. Web. 30 Sept. 2015. <http://www.nsf.gov/pubs/2005/nsb0540/nsb0540.pdf>.

[53] Prewitt, Kenneth; Mackie, Christopher D.; Habermann, Hermann, *Civic Engagement and Social Cohesion: Measuring Dimensions of Social Capital to Inform Policy*. National Academies Press, 2014.

[54] Manyika, James; Chui, Michael; Brown, Brad; Bughin, Jacques; Dobbs, Richard; Roxburgh, Charles; Byers, Angela Hung. "Big data: The next frontier for innovation, competition, and productivity." *McKinsey Global Institute*. <http://www.mckinsey.com/insights/business_technology/big_data_the_next_frontier_for_innovation>.

[55] "Training Students to Extract Value From Big Data: Summary of a Workshop." *National Research Council of The National Academies*. (2014). Web. 30 Sept. 2015. <http://www.nap.edu/openbook.php?record_id=18981>.

[56] "Big Data to Knowledge (BD2K)." *National Institutes of Health*. Web. 30 Sept. 2015. <https://datascience.nih.gov/bd2k>.

[57] "Investing in Science, Engineering, and Education for the Nation's Future: Strategic Plan for 2014-2018." *National Science Foundation*. Web. 30 Sept. 2015. <http://www.nsf.gov/pubs/2014/nsf14043/nsf14043.pdf>.

[58] "Training Students to Extract Value From Big Data: Summary of a Workshop." *National Research Council of The National Academies*. (2014). Web. 30 Sept. 2015. <http://www.nap.edu/openbook.php?record_id=18981>.